D1414029

COSTLY
PERFORMANCES

COSTLY
PERFORMANCES

Tennessee Williams: The Last Stage

Bruce Smith

PARAGON HOUSE
NEW YORK

First edition, 1990

Published in the United States by
Paragon House
90 Fifth Avenue
New York, NY
10011

Copyright © Bruce Smith, 1990

Library of Congress Cataloging-in-Publication Data

Smith, Bruce (James Bruce)
Costly performances : Tennessee Williams : the last stage / by
Bruce Smith.
        p.   cm.
        ISBN 1-55778-175-3
    1. Williams, Tennessee, 1911–1983—Biography.
                    2. Dramatists,
American—20th century—Biography.   I. Title.
            PS3545.I5365Z835   1990
                812'.54—dc20
    [B]   89-29444
                                            CIP

"Vincent (Starry, Starry Night)" words and music by Don
McLean © copyright 1971, 1972 by Music Corporation of
America, Inc. and Benny Bird Music. Rights administered
by MCA Music Publishing, a division of MCA, Inc., 1755
Broadway, New York, N.Y. 10019. Used by permission. All
rights reserved.

The paper used in this publication meets the minimum
requirements of American National Standard for Information
Sciences—Permanence of Paper for Printed Library Materials,
ANSI Z39.48-1984.

For the Smith family: My mother, Jane; my sister Susan and my father, James B. And for these friends, cast in order of appearance upon the stage of my life: Zella Wolson, Henry Rago, Dean M. Lierle, Jr., Howard E. Weatherly, William R. Brown, Nigel John Sandor and, still haunting the triumphant trove of the Newberry Library, Stanley and Mabel Pargellis.

In Memoriam, Ian Charleson, actor, whose own chariot of fire brought Tennessee a "Cat" he would believe.

"And so it came about that . . . I was unjustly accused of being a politician, because I was privy to the secret griefs of wild unknown men."

—F. Scott Fitzgerald
The Great Gatsby

COSTLY
PERFORMANCES

PERSPECTIVE

———————⟨≈⟩———————

IT IS ONLY APPROPRIATE to set the stage for a book called *Costly Performances*. Necessary to understand the personal drama of this production are perhaps three keys: the Janus key—personal life (face), dramatic side (reverse); brief provenance of the protagonist's origins and name; revelation of achievement.

That Tennessee was active in the creation of his persona and fame from an early time is not to be doubted. The name by which he would become known to the world was seized from the top of the family tree. Tennessee was the site of all of the antecedent Williams heroes. On the father's side we have Tennessee's first senator and the brother of the State's first governor. Many, in their early innocence, had fought the Indians for the land. Sevier was the surname of that first governor and Sevier was the Huguenots rendering of the Roman Catholic Xavier, whose most illustrious forebear was the St. Francis of that name. The man whom, as

Tennessee observed, was "credited with the Quixotic con-
version of many Chinese—a questionably valiant under-
taking, in my opinion."

Tennessee, then, was a name associated with valor and
some accomplishment. The two states from which Tennessee Williams actually came were Mississippi and Missouri,
hardly candidates for given names of theatrical resonance.

Born in Columbus, Mississippi, on March 26, 1911, St.
Louis was the crucible of Tennessee's creative life. There in
the reduced circumstances and foreign urban decline in
which the future writer found himself, he lived with his
mother, Edwina, and his sister, Rose. The father, Cornelius
Coffin Williams, was the classically distant parent, deaf to
his son's sensitivities, perhaps even more so once his left ear
was bitten off in a barroom brawl.

This crucible created the major personae of the Williams
dramatic legacy throughout his years of major achievement. The mother, Edwina, became Amanda in Tennessee's
first great recognized play, *The Glass Menagerie,* as did Rose
become Laura. Tom is Tom in that production, but as his
own personality developed, foundered and reasserted itself
through the years, Tennessee was represented by many an
interesting avatar, from the basic writer-son in *Menagerie*
through the Princess Kosmonopolis in *Sweet Bird of Youth.*
Blanche du Bois of *A Streetcar Named Desire* was, of course,
his most famous and internationally notorious feminine
incarnation. Italian director Luchino Visconti openly referred to Tennessee as Blanche during the Roman production of *Streetcar.*

Tennessee's sister, Rose, has entered the pantheon of
great female American archetypes most forcibly, perhaps,
because her own real life was snapped off by her own
mother early on in her development. Rose, carrying the
Williams sensitivity and withdrawal from "reality" to what

were considered excessive heights by the standards of St. Louis society in the 30's, was lobotomized. In consequence, she has lived, as schizophrenics are said to do, two lives. One, principally at Stony Lodge Asylum in Upstate New York. The other very much alive and out there upon the boards in everything from *Menagerie* to *Summer and Smoke* to *Suddenly Last Summer* to *The Two Character Play.*

Of notable exception to such dramatic usage of family members are brother Dakin, whose dramatic appearances were confined to real life and Tennessee's father, Cornelius, who makes an eponymous appearance in Tennessee's last play, *A House Not Meant to Stand.*

Through the years, this matching of family archetypes with the characters in Williams's plays will undoubtedly become an academic discipline, perhaps as early as the big biography now accumulating in Austin. But this brief history indicates Tennessee's traditional source of dramatic usage. What he couldn't find in the family, he made from the stuff and personalities of the life about him.

Because *Costly Performances* is a personal memoir, I must add my own to explication of this playwriting mode. Of all the emotions evoked by the many inscriptions Tennessee left behind for me in my library of his books, none is more telling or more moving than this (on the flyleaf of *The Glass Menagerie*): "For you (Bruce) and Amanda (Edwina), Love, Tennessee."

What to make of it? I make this: Throughout the years, as I have said, all his characters were based on persons closely associated with him in life. These persons formed his personal mythos. In fact, as is revealed in this book, Tennessee's last great play was the life he lived in his last years, with the later plays mere reflections of his then ending days.

So, after nearly a decade, the message becomes clear and

it becomes the legend above the door to this book. Edwina, his mother, was the source, as said, for the mother in his first successful play, *The Glass Menagerie*. I, by a sheer chance of meeting that happened, as he often said "to touch his soul," became both person and persona for some of the last enactments of his career. This is a personal key to his creativity and one which I feel privileged to have been given, even if in so casual a fashion as a message in an inscribed book.

This key further illuminates the mission he set for me. Although Tennessee fought fiercely for the production of his final works (which were produced in the time I knew him), he seemed also to know that his final work, now so closely honed to his day-to-day life, might well escape recording if he did not find some final friend to whom he could say: "If you can realize a book from this experience, do it. I've been talking about a rather black sequel to my *Memoirs,* but I know I'll never do it. . . ." The actual experience is recalled in the pages to come, but some further enhancement may well prove helpful. I can still see him as he says these words. He had chosen the location as a scene of celebrity: Booth One of The Pump Room of the Ambassador East in Chicago. Most often, he chose the other route: escape from the public eye. But this night must have the appropriate set, so: "Let's go to the The Pump Room tonight. And don't be discreet. Tell them I want Booth One." A symbol carefully chosen for the celebrity he so often shunned, but it would be a mistake to forget the satisfactions he did really find in his own celebrity. This book may disclose his sad, last decline, but the details of that disclosure are bereft of full meaning if the almost always thwarted heights are not revealed. Tennessee knew his symbols would work as persuasively on me as they worked for the audiences of his plays. "Write the truth of all this ugly time," he was saying, "but let's not forget Booth One!"

It is in the true tradition of bold Tennessee Williams irony that this book was written under conditions similar to those under which he wrought his own *Memoirs:* the troubled production of a play, in that case *Small Craft Warnings.* It is not as though warnings, pertaining to small craft and otherwise, were not cordially extended in his *Memoirs.* But no one expected a follow-up. Although he could no longer do it, he found a writer who would attend him during the production of his last works. He encouraged *Costly Performances* as a follow-up to his own *Memoirs.*

As I have suggested, Tennessee Williams courted, crafted and created his own celebrity. Of course, it was his genius which swept him to the pinnacle of great twentieth century playwrights and that process was begun in the city where it would end, Chicago. Here, in 1944, *The Glass Menagerie* was mounted. By name and by sentiment it was about as fragile a vessel as possible to set upon the troubled waters of a world fraught with war, but the gentle flame held long enough for it to catch fire, due largely to the handsome, deft critical support of the *Chicago Tribune's* Claudia Cassidy. Her reviews of the play numbered more than one. It was her inspired comparison of the play's star, Laurette Taylor, with the legendary Eleanora Duse that may well have finally caught the public's imagination. The words stirred the nation's entire critical fraternity to venture into wintry Chicago. And so it arrived on Broadway on March 31, 1945 to national critical acclaim.

Tennessee's first published response to success was prophetic. An essay published in the *New York Times* after *Menagerie* had opened was called "The Catastrophe of Success." It confided that the rapid change of lifestyle occasioned by the success of *Menagerie* was one of disorienting contrast. Denying that the kind of success measured by lavish hotel suites and hoards of uninvited attendees was the furthest from his ambitions, he reminds his readers that he has had a life of "required endurance, a life of clawing and scratching along a sheer surface and holding on tight with raw fingers to every inch of rock higher than the one caught hold of before. . . ." But, he importantly reminds us (and this is crucial to an understanding of his life and particularly that which is chronicled in the following pages): "It was a good life because it was the sort of life for which the human organism is created."

Tennessee would remain so (that is to say, elementally Darwinian) to the end of his days. He thrived on emotional and environmental chaos, savoring his own man-made jungle to the contemporary corporate world gone bland with incremental and fundamentally uninspired accomplishment. The jungle would always be essential and he made that existential decision quite early in his career. Soon after the Broadway opening of *Menagerie,* he packed his bags with only minimal provisions and fled to Mexico, "an elemental country where you can quickly forget the false dignities and conceits imposed by success." He had jettisoned what he came to call, during our time together, "Uptown Shit," and went to Mexico to work on his next (and many consider his greatest) play, *A Streetcar Named Desire.*

This approach/avoidance syndrome was acted out throughout Williams's life. He both courted fame and, at the same time, regarded success as a threat to his elemental creative self—and so a "catastrophe." For those who did live within the decades when the name Tennessee Williams was synonymous with the greatest contemporary drama (far eclipsing O'Neill and Miller), it is important to remember that he was probably the most rewarded playwright of his age. In his late life his incarnation was perceived as largely that of the pariah. But during his great decades, no playwright enjoyed in such quantity the awards, the celebrity status and friends, the cults of sychophants, the phalanx of stars who owed him their careers, the substantial financial rewards.

His absorption with this theme of retaining his elemental self sought further expression. He would soon add, to this earlier declaration: "Security is a kind of death, I think, and it can come to you in a storm of royalty checks beside a kidney-shaped pool in Beverly Hills or anywhere at all that is removed from the conditions that made you an artist, if that's what you were intended to be." Tennessee, always uncertain as to the source of his genius, guarded its presumed well-springs jealously, frantically. Because of this, comfort would seldom come to him, nor to those who knew him intimately. As roiling with psychic tension, terror and sometimes physical violence as his plays were, he saw the source of these visions as life itself. And, the father of the play, life, must remain even more terrible, violent and tense than the plays themselves.

Costly Performances will reveal one great, occasional prick to the tension: humor. For Tennessee was wildly endowed with this necessary psychic emollient. Dark, guarded, ferocious, cunning, lively, always on, his humor. Frequent examples enliven the incidents to come in these pages.

Another important insight to insert here: Tennessee's approach/avoidance lifestyle lost him the opportunity of ever forming about him a constant, nurturing coterie of like-minded friends, such as we presume possible in other cultures. Surely, we know enough of Harold Pinter and his world to assume he lives in such a group. And, importantly, it was that other St. Louis writer of another generation, T.S. Eliot, who sought and found the cultural and emotional climate he required on a sustained basis in England. But though, in time, Tennessee's international theatre connections would afford him ample opportunity to form such sustaining connections, he never did so. It was his mission to stay faithful to the American heart alone in all its troubled life.

But some kind of tenuous community of spirit was inevitable as Tennessee's life became increasingly enriched by the success of his work. Though he had fled to Mexico during the run of *Menagerie,* the theatre world marked this initial bow of his upon the international stage with its New York Drama Critics Award. And, on a personal basis, *Menagerie's* star, Laurette Taylor, was Tennessee's first association with the great of the theatre world. In his *Memoirs,* he says of her that it was her performance as Amanda that assured the play's success; that she was a gallant performer and that she was the greatest artist of her profession that he had ever known (and this was said after he had known them all). Here it may be seen that, though Tennessee, so short a time before, was only clinging to the surface of life's steep inclinations "with raw fingers," he was reaching for and, indeed, capturing the stars in very short order.

That his first flight from the horrors of Manhattan celebrity to the elemental style of Mexico was not entirely in the spirit of Graham Greene's *The Power and the Glory* (written just a few years previously) we may take for granted as we see him disporting himself with Leonard Bernstein in Mexico City. Though this particular association was not to flourish, it was an early indicator of Tennessee's admittance into the international (though still somewhat discreet) world of high rollers (earned, we may say, by sheer dint of genius and effort) which would include Christopher Isherwood, Gore Vidal, Truman Capote, Samuel Barber, Gian Carlo Menotti and a coterie of others of a perhaps lesser luminescent sphere. At thirty-four, Tennessee was of an international artistic rank. And this rank advanced steadily, incrementally, geometrically until the 1960's, when sheer creative exhaustion was further exacerbated by the severance of the long sustained love and support of his friend, Frank Merlo, whose place in Tennessee's life is accounted for just ahead.

Despite the oft-recounted hellish side of Tennessee's later life, there were the clear and open early years, when success delivered her promise of pleasure with an open hand. In those years, Tennessee revelled, indeed. His recounted memories of his summers in Rome in the late 1940's are those of a very happy man, seldom divided against himself. There is an early image of him as he races at dawn, round and round the fountains in Vatican Square in his open car, the waters cool and perhaps even spiritual by association, spraying him awake to a new day of pleasure in post-war Italy, where Americans were welcome, whatever their persuasion. He recounts his Chaplinesque encounters with the highly romantic, highly indigent youths of the Via Veneto and, later, the high times with Anna Magnani, her lovers, her dogs, her memorable disapproval of his penchant for Scotch so late at night. These were high and happy times to be remembered to balance the weight of the last, sad years recorded here.

The years 1947 and 1948 intertwine to become the most benign of double helixes, years when *A Streetcar Named Desire* swept aside all previous records of critical acclaim and commercial success and when Tennessee finally secured a personal alliance at once nurturing and secure.

When *Streetcar* opened on Broadway at the Barrymore Theatre on December 3, 1947 (with Marlon Brando as Stanley and Jessica Tandy as Blanche), a storm of critical acclaim arose which carried the play from Broadway to the cross-continental U.S., to England, France, Italy, Germany, Greece, Austria, Uruguay, Holland, Norway, Sweden, Denmark, Switzerland and Poland. Thereafter, it was presented in the Soviet Union, which initiated Russia to a taste for Williams which makes him the most produced playwright in that country, perhaps the unlikely harbinger of glasnost! During its first year of presentation, *Streetcar* won for Williams the Pulitzer Prize, the Donaldson Award and the New York Drama Critics Award. No less an American sensitive than William Rose Benet said of *Streetcar:* "This is one of the most remarkable plays of our time. It is native tragedy, written by one who is both poet and first-rate dramatist. On re-reading, it reveals increasing richness of connotation."

But, while the play soared to unprecedented heights of acclaim and fortune, contemporary greats like Laurence Olivier were hesitant about touching it. Olivier's wife at that time, the great Vivien Leigh (one of Tennessee's most loved performers, personally and professionally), wanted desperately to do Blanche, with her husband to direct. Olivier allowed as how he "was hesitant about this work, owing to my not quite dead preoccupation with respectability."

Streetcar did open in London, under Olivier's direction, on October 11, 1949. Vivien Leigh was a sensational Blanche. She had the imagination to coarsen her lovely Southern accent (as developed for her role as Scarlett O'Hara in *Gone With the Wind*) as a nice theatrical touch and the result was electrifying. This performance has been captured in the Warner Brothers film, for which she won her second Academy Award. Later, when it came time for Olivier to write his *Confessions of an Actor,* in 1982, he referred to *Streetcar* as "that great play." Olivier had unstrung his own hypocrisy through the years, as had most of the theatrical world. Blanche remains one of the most coveted roles in the twentieth century repertoire and Marlon Brando correctly avers that it was his Stanley that gained him almost immediate stature as the leading American actor of his day. *Streetcar* also marked the beginning of Tennessee's tremendously productive creative association with Elia Kazan, who directed the premier production.

Meanwhile, Tennessee's life was stretched between the dark bedrooms of his desire and the relentless streetcar of his fame, which was hurtling him into the pitched camps of the world's great centers and their theatres. With the perfect timing that asserts itself without pause in his plays, Tennessee now, in 1948, at the height of his fame, quite spontaneously fell in love with an honest, natively intelligent, attractive and unbeglamored young man named Frank Merlo. Though Tennessee had met Merlo some months earlier on the Cape, Frank had not pursued the acquaintance, because, as he said when the two met by chance some months later in Manhattan, "I don't like to climb on band-wagons. When you hit it big with *Streetcar* last year, I figured you'd think I just wanted to exploit a little meeting we'd had on a beach. That's why I never got in touch with you. But I saw the play and loved it."

Frank Merlo then assumed a role from which he was not to emerge alive. This level-headed youth from New Jersey became a kind of physio-psychic gyroscope for the increasingly erratic Williams voyage through fame and fortune. They established a rather fond menage in an unpretentious house on Duncan Street in Key West. It was to that home that Tennessee would turn for space to breathe as well as for human warmth and comfort. It was in these years with Merlo, between *Streetcar* in 1947 and *The Night of the Iguana* in 1961 that Tennessee tore up the American map and formula for theatrical success and remade it very much in his own image. It was during these productive years that he offered us a clearer view of the contemporary human condition, an acceptance of its limitations, a love and caring for its brief visions. Tennessee's epigraph for *Streetcar* is from Hart Crane's *The Broken Tower:*

> *And so it was I entered the broken world*
> *To trace the visionary company of love, its voice*
> *An instant in the wind (I know not whither hurled)*
> *But not for long to hold each desperate choice.*

Lines quoted before Frank, after whom each choice became, for more than a decade, less desperate and the company of love less visionary and very much more real.

Tennessee's next play was *Summer and Smoke,* which, when initially presented on Broadway in 1948, was not well received. At the end of the play's premier, Tennessee turned to his partner for the evening's entertainment, Carson McCullers, and said, "Let's get out of here," a turn of phrase familiar through the years at the end of almost all the openings of Tennessee's plays. (I was perhaps the last to hear them, as the curtain fell on his last play in Chicago, the ill-omened *A House Not Meant to Stand.*) The next morning, McCullers sought to comfort Tennessee with perfectly brewed coffee and the soothing strains of a Mozart quartet. It was Frank Merlo's first chance to assert his effective self. He politely showed Carson to a cab, roused Tennessee from his bed and got him back to his typewriter, which was the only true comfort Tennessee knew when confronted with criticism he thought unfair.

Later, in 1952, the re-worked *Summer and Smoke* was to occasion the birth of Off-Broadway, when Jose Quintero directed a production of the play at the Circle in the Square. This was the debut of Geraldine Page in Tennessee's works. She makes some interesting appearances here, in *Costly Performances,* not all of them pleasant bows. However, Quintero and the New York critics found her "incandescent." Brooks Atkinson, drama critic for the *New York Times,* reviewing it for the paper, said: "Nothing more momentous has happened in the theatre in the last few years than the revival of *Summer and Smoke* at the new off-Broadway theatre called Circle in the Square."

It was this production that made the reputations of the theatre, the director and the star. However, that star, Ms. Page, would undo herself, in the estimation of many, when after a year with the play, she signed for an immediate Broadway production, informing no one involved at Circle with her intent. Her method of disengaging herself was effective. She ran through an entire night's performance of *Summer and Smoke* in half the time it required. Wringing her hands in her dressing room after her last performance, she explained her rushed job was the best way she could think of to make everyone at the theatre honestly hate her so that she could take on her next coveted role with a clear conscience! It did the trick for Quintero. He fired her on the spot.

Just after the first, unappreciated *Summer and Smoke,* Tennessee offered up to the theatre world *The Rose Tattoo,* which opened at Broadway's Martin Beck Theatre on February 3, 1951. This play was, in Tennessee's words, "My love play to the world." He went on to say: "It was permeated with my love for Frankie and I dedicated it to him." The play was previewed in Chicago, where the largely faithful Claudia Cassidy, though not knowing quite what to do with it after *Menagerie* and *Streetcar,* still gave it a good review.

Appropriately, as indicated by its dedicatee, the play was an "allegory of sexual power," according to Harold Clurman, who was an often sensitive guide to Tennessee's work, a fact which was to be rewarded in 1957, when Tennessee named him director of his play for that year, *Orpheus Descending*. Reviews for *Tattoo* were decidedly mixed and Tennessee, in his emerging tradition, fled the city for Key West. It was there that a kind of salvation for the play came along, in the unlikely guise of the young Gore Vidal. Peddling on his bike to the Williams compound, he told Tennessee upon arrival that he was a special friend of Marion Davies, who was the "special friend" of that grand media mogul, William Randolph Hearst. Vidal suggested that Tennessee autograph his complete published works and send them off to Marion as soon as possible. This early assay in p.r. worked, for shortly thereafter favorable features on *Tattoo,* its author and cast appeared in all the papers of the Hearst syndicate. The national media fervor created welcome lines at the Martin Beck box office.

The *Rose Tattoo* saga, behind the scenes, was star-crossed. Tennessee had wanted Anna Magnani, the great Italian actress, for the U.S. stage production and, indeed, had written the role specifically for her. But her English, she felt, was not up to nightly live performances. Certain persons, interested in the advancement of the career of the young Maureen Stapleton, suggested her for the role of the heroine of the play, Serafina, despite her seeming inappropriateness for the role. She was so young, she could scarcely have copulated the four thousand-plus times Serafina boasts she had with her late husband. The spirit of Procrustes, shaping form to need, was summoned by the production staff, ruffling-up, be-smearing and generally dressing-down the young actress. As recounted in this book, Stapleton may well have had her revenge at Tennessee's last Broadway birthday party. She is seen there attacking his birthday cake with a butcher's knife.

Magnani did make the film version of *Tattoo*, which was filmed close to the author's Key West home, with Burt Lancaster her co-star. Tennessee's summation of her work in the film, "She was magnificent!"

With the critical and commercial success of film versions of both *Streetcar* and *Tattoo*, Tennessee was now known to an even wider international audience. What was perhaps the apotheosis of his career would come in 1954 with the enraptured world response to *Cat on a Hot Tin Roof*, but before that great success came the problematical *Camino Real*, a play so different from Tennessee's almost perfectly Aristotelian creations that audiences had a hard time apprehending it. Elia Kazan would direct this difficult play, which would pre-figure many later play production methods, most notably the notion of having the cast move out among the audience as a means of involvement. *Camino Real*, presented on Broadway in 1953, at the National Theatre, ran less than two months. Kazan on *Camino* is revealing: "*Camino Real* is an imperfect play, but it is beautiful, a love letter to the people Williams loved most, the romantics, those innocents who became victims in our business civilization . . . here, waiting for the end, are the high fliers Tennessee cherished: Jacques Casanova, Don Quixote, Marguerite, la Dame aux Camelias, the Baron du Charlus. They are all doomed, but Kilroy (the hero), has a quality the others have lost; he can still struggle to get up when he's knocked down." Tennessee would have ample opportunity to play at Kilroy during the decade to come, the emotionally unravelling 60's.

With this view of *Camino*, it is not surprising to reflect that, during his last years, Tennessee almost always spoke to me of *Camino* as a work closest to his inner vision. He often underscored a point he wished to make by quoting from the play and lines from it had assumed the authority

of something of an anthem for his last years, when he had
come to the place described in the play's production notes:
"a final mysterious place, where Death waits." In his own
notes on the play, Tennessee observes: "My desire was to
give these audiences my own sense of something wild and
unrestricted that ran like water in the mountains, or clouds
changing shape in a gale, or the continually dissolving and
transforming images of a dream."

It is more than an important theatrical footnote to recall
that *Camino Real* was a production of the Actors Studio, an
organization that did much to advance the American theatre world on Broadway during its great days of the 40's
and 50's. With every professional assist behind it, however,
as observed, it escaped critical understanding. His constant affirmations in his late years that *Camino* was a great
play, was always accompanied by the admission that he had
written it under the stimulation of speed (amphetamines).
I always took this to imply his valiant assertion that he
could write great work no matter what chemicals were
astream through his body. Another touching aspect of
Camino recall was the almost votive use to which he would
put inscriptions from the work in books he autographed for
friends. His motto was from the work and it was always:
"Make voyages. Attempt things. There is nothing else."

To note an alpha and omega effect: The final big play of
Tennessee's career, *Clothes for A Summer Hotel,* was also
written in a time warp as fluid as a Dali watch. It, like
Camino, escaped adequate appreciation. America seemed to
want him firmly in the Aristotelian mode. When he abandoned it, his audiences abandoned him.

Kazan's lonely affirmation of *Camino* was rewarded with
the directorship of what Tennessee always called his favorite
play, *Cat on a Hot Tin Roof.* The initial 1954 production of
Cat was a battle of wits and wills between the playwright

and director. Kazan saw the young Barbara Bel Geddes as a perfect Maggie the Cat, but Tennessee did not concur. As for the director's choice for Big Daddy, Burl Ives, Tennessee could only observe with undeniable lucidity: "He's a singer, isn't he?" Ben Gazzara, as the problematical Brick, was accepted without undue scepticism.

But the creative conflict between writer and director resulted in what was probably the greatest dramatic success that ever hit Broadway. Within short order, it was given both that year's Pulitzer Prize and the New York Drama Critics Award. It was made into a commercially successful film version starring Elizabeth Taylor and Paul Newman. Laurence Olivier directed an interesting version of it for Britain's Granada Television.

Success or not, Tennessee once again "fled the city," this time to Rome, where he experienced an unsettling onset of writer's block. His antidote: a Seconal washed down with a dry martini. Whatever the recipe, he managed to produce the script for what would become *Baby Doll,* the 1956 film which produced an inter-denominational furor of unprecedented proportions. The National Legion of Decency banned it among its legionnaires as "morally repellant both in theme and treatment," since it dwelt "almost without variation or relief upon carnal suggestiveness in action, dialogue and costuming." Cardinal Spellman, about whom Tennessee could be most amusing in private, condemned it from the pulpit of St. Patrick's Cathedral. All the squalid moral fuss of the 50's killed its box office. Today it could be played on prime time television without demur.

In 1957, that theatrical personage with a refined social conscience, Harold Clurman, was given the opportunity to direct the initial Broadway production of *Orpheus Descending.* It starred, once again, the reliable Magnani stand-in, Maureen Stapleton (Tennessee had written the starring role of Lady Torrance for Anna Magnani, who managed to star in the later film version of *Orpheus*, retitled *The Fugitive Kind*) and the young Cliff Robertson. Of its distinct critical failure, Tennessee was to say, simply, "It was under-directed." Today, in 1989, *Orpheus Descending* has just come to Broadway with Vanessa Redgrave in the lead as Lady. The reviews now are more than marginal, suggesting that Tennessee's world view of the human condition is more prevalent and so more acceptable to the audience of today.

The year 1958 saw the twin production of *Garden District*, the comprehensive title under which two new plays were offered: *Something Unspoken* and *Suddenly Last Summer*. Tennessee had chosen the "gifted and amusing" Herbert Machiz to direct. Opening at The York Theatre on January 7, 1958, it received rave reviews. The film version of *Suddenly Last Summer*, which Tennessee disliked as a film but approved of as a profitable venture, has become something of a cult classic, largely because of the extraordinary dialog delivered by Katherine Hepburn as Mrs. Venable. Tennessee later observed that he thought *Suddenly* contained some of his best writing.

The Martin Beck Theatre was the venue for the 1959 production of Tennessee's play for that year, *Sweet Bird of Youth*. Under the creative directorship of Elia Kazan, *Bird* was the occasion of yet another creative conflict between the playwright and director. Kazan's vision was clear. Alexandra del Lago (the faded star) was Tennessee incarnate, in his own self-vision. Tennessee took exception to Kazan's view of him, as Alexandra del Lago, as a "mean, alcoholic bitch." This interpretation would often twinge the playwright in later years, because, he would admit, "It came too close to the truth in those years."

In any event, the play opened to rave reviews, with the often difficult Kenneth Tynan saying of the still unforgiven

Geraldine Page, "She acted with knock-down flamboyance and drag-out authority." The play was a great commercial success and, with that in mind, MGM secured the film rights. That film, retaining the major stars, was a sheer travesty of Tennessee's intent and he never forgave Hollywood for it.

In 1960, Tennessee Williams's Broadway offering was *Period of Adjustment,* which opened November 10 at the Helen Hayes Theatre and was directed by George Roy Hill. This production is of some historical significance in that it signals Tennessee's break with Elia Kazan, who had chosen to direct the new William Inge play that year rather than Tennessee's more problematical work. Tennessee harbored his resentment for years, despite the fact that the Hill production enjoyed some measure of critical success. In general, the critical summation was that it was not Tennessee in top form, but all were amazed that he had written what was as close to a light comedy as he could manage. The much admired Brooks Atkinson, ever the critical Polonius, observed: "[*Period of Adjustment*] is so far below Mr. Williams's standard that it proves nothing one way or the other. His heart is not in that mediocre jest."

The sheer weight of productivity would begin to bear down on Tennessee after the combined onslaught of the national tour of the big play for 1961: *The Night of the Iguana* and the death of Frank Merlo at the end of this period. *Iguana* opened on December 18, 1961 at the Royale Theatre, starring Bette Davis and Margaret Leighton. The cross fire between these two was something to see and Davis, who was making her stage comeback with this play, was unstoppable in her ambition. She even managed to fire Tennessee's carefully chosen director, Frank Corsaro, in Chicago, before the Broadway opening. Entering the winter of his discontent, Tennessee once again sensed a doomed

production, but was surprised by the warm welcome critical response *Iguana* received. Though Claudia Cassidy, who
had really given him his start back in Chicago in 1944
with *Menagerie* termed *Iguana* "bankrupt" in her review, the
New York critics were positive in their assessment and for
it Tennessee received his fourth Drama Critics Circle
Award. It was later made into a film of some notoriety,
starring Richard Burton, Ava Gardner and Deborah Kerr.
The rights for this work were in some dispute, according to
Tennessee, and a minor uproar erupts on the subject in the
forthcoming pages.

The success with *Night of the Iguana* was really the
figurative and actual capstone of Tennessee's career. From
1962, when he broke with Frank Merlo because of what a
mutual friend, Paul Bigelow, described as a diversity of
lifestyles (presumably, Tennessee's becoming more aristo-
cratic and less confined and Frank's adherence to the mod-
eration of a lower middle class homelife) and then, within a
year, Frank's death, Tennessee went on into the decade
when, he said "I was always falling down and nobody
picked me up." His last big deal from that period was an
enormously ill-conceived and executed production of *The
Milk Train Doesn't Stop Here Anymore.* Tallulah Bankhead
had forced her way into it, the director, Tony Richardson
(of *Tom Jones* fame) had insisted on co-starring Tab Hunter
and Tennessee was far from in control. The 1963 production closed after five performances. But, in an ominous note
sounding for the forseeable future, *Milk Train* was rendered
down into the film *Boom!*, starring the then Burtons,
Richard and Elizabeth. With the aged Noel Coward in
black tie green with age, the film became an instant camp
hit. No one, least of all Tennessee himself, seemed to know
what to do with Tennessee's new work anymore.

By all contemporary accounts it was the death of Frank

Merlo in 1963 which precipitated Tennessee's major break-down then, emotionally and physically, and so there is a kind of professional drought throughout the mid and late 60's, with the exceptions noted below. While friends could choose to draw a discreet (if abhorrently Victorian) curtain over much of his behind the scenes activity of this period, it has been more than drawn and quartered in two recent books, unnamed here for matters of taste and for matters of respect for their subject. It should be observed, however, that Tennessee began the public effort of published defa-mation by publishing his own *Memoirs* in 1975. With these, he cast in bronze what had been but shadowy suspi-cion among the hoi-polloi and the haute monde prior to its publication. Now, of course, we are grateful for this book, which captures so much of Tennessee's charm of observa-tion, his humor and his blatant honesty. At the time, however, the book contributed to his general unbank-ability and helped to retard the personal renascence he had envisioned for himself when I first met him in 1979.

By the mid 60's the great participators in new works by Tennessee Williams had begun to dwindle. The ever-gallant Margaret Leighton was drawn into a 1966 produc-tion called *Slapstick Tragedy,* Tennessee's first attempt at broad black humor. The reviews were uniformly unsym-pathetic, as they were to revivals of some of this material (published in the collection *Dragon Country*) described in some detail in this book.

The year 1968 saw the Broadway production of *The Seven Descents of Myrtle,* directed by Jose Quintero and starring Estelle Parsons. The critics savaged it and it closed within the month.

The world of *Dragon Country* reached its 60's apotheosis with the 1969 production *In the Bar of a Tokyo Hotel,* which opened at New York's Eastside Playhouse on May 11,

1969, starring Anne Meacham and Donald Madden. Of this production, Tennessee's mother, Edwina, who had travelled to New York for the opening, observed: "Tom, it is time you found another occupation now." *New York Times* critic Clive Barnes had another thought about this production, however. He observed: "A simple phrase such as 'a diaphanous afternoon in August floats across like summer smoke' or 'an artist has to lay his life on the line.' (indicate) there are more flashes of genius here than in any of his later plays." On an optimistic note, he foretold: "Like *Camino Real, Tokyo Bar* is avant garde and will be appreciated and applauded in the theatre of the future."

Only two new plays during the 70's would occupy the nation's attention to Tennessee's theatrical output. One was *Out Cry,* which had gone through several incarnations, first as *The Two Character Play* (in 1967, in London, then as *Out Cry* in Chicago, 1971) and then in New York at the Lyceum Theatre in 1973, starring Michael York, for whom Tennessee always held high hopes for an outstanding career in the theatre. The reviews were lame. It was revived again in New York on August 14, 1975, again with unsupportive notices. This play was especially close to Tennessee's heart throughout his later life and it is of high interest to note that he bequeathed the royalties from this incestuous drama to Maria St. Just, who figures so colorfully in the pages to come.

Before the pages of this book open in 1979 with the advent of Tennessee's last big play, *Clothes for a Summer Hotel,* his major project was the play *Small Craft Warnings* on which he was working at the time he composed his *Memoirs,* published in 1975. After that, there had been a short-lived production of a play called *Vieux Carre,* produced in New York at The St. James Theatre in 1977. Just prior to that, in 1976, there was the production of *Eccen-*

tricities of a Nightingale, which was in some ways an earlier version of *Summer and Smoke.* New York Times critic Clive Barnes liked it better than *Summer and Smoke* as it had originally appeared and commented, "It is a rich, warm play (with) Mr. Williams at his shining, gentle best." The date is important. It was his last good Broadway notice.

For purposes of historical accuracy, I wish to note that there was a production of a play more or less simultaneous with the ones mentioned in *Costly Performances.* That was *Something Cloudy, Something Clear,* produced at the Jean Cocteau Repertory Theatre in New York, August, 1981 through March, 1982. Tennessee had worked on it during the run of *Clothes for a Summer Hotel,* with a working title, *The Silver Victrola.* It was a rendering of his first relationship with another man, the Kip of his *Memoirs.* His personal involvement with this production was quite minimal, his energies being addressed to the Goodman Theatre productions described herein.

These theatrical notes do not mean, in any sense, to cover with total comprehensiveness the entirety of Tennessee Williams's play production. During the late years, there were productions of Tennessee's plays almost anywhere anyone had thought to provide a stage. But they do bring to light for a new generation the enormity of his fame and his creation of and contribution to what is the greatest of American theatre.

And, for that newer generation, one might ask: "Just how contemporary does he play?" Turn then to the present day production of *Orpheus Descending* on Broadway. One character, Carol Cutrere, stylized once as a "Christ-bitten reformer," has now abandoned that career as hopeless and has been identified by the local constabulary as a "lewd vagrant." She says, with an eloquence that echoes the soul of Tennessee Williams down through all his days of observation and creation: "Something is wild in the country. This country used to be wild, the men and women were wild and there was a wild sort of sweetness in their hearts for each other, but, now, it's sick with neon, like most other places . . ."

We need only remember that Tennessee preferred fire to neon and that with that element he did the Promethean as a playwright: He searched for and held up for us to see the scorching divisions of the human heart.

Bruce Smith
Chicago, 1989

CHAPTER I

The Tiger in the Tiger Pit

"T.S. ELIOT: THAT EVITIATED versifier!" was Tennessee's resounding commentary on his fellow St. Louis poet/playwright. Yet, Eliot certainly had the current word on Tennessee's condition. In his "Lines for an Old Man" he may have foreseen Tennessee when he wrote: "The tiger in the tiger pit is not more irritable than I." Lines onward in the poem referring to enemies writhing in essential blood may apply as well. But let Tennessee speak in his own words. It is early January 1980.

"Morphine! My brother most recently has taken to accusing me, in a highly public manner, of being a morphine addict. Such, I believe, may have been the quiet custom of some antebellum ladies of his acquaintance, but this addiction does not apply to me. Can you even imagine a morphine addict? A further declension of drug addict and alcoholic. Now, a newer charge is that I'm illiterate. Yes, baby, that's the newest charge, I'm illiterate! I'm certain

the *New York Times* came up with that one. According to
them, I'm the most illiterate major writer in America.
Drunk, drugged, and illiterate and you ask why I don't
leave Key West. Well, they don't know it yet, baby, but I
am leaving Key West and I'm leaving for the Kennedy
Center in Washington, D.C. I've got a big new play and
I'm going to town with it."

Our evening had begun earlier, amid the dark foliage
and bamboo chairs of a bar on Key West's main drag, Duval
Street. I had seen him emerge from the jungle foliage of
the bar's garden and take a seat much by himself. As I
approached him for our pre-dinner drink, I reflected that
I did not disdain him, unlike the local conchs and Manhattan snowbirds who encountered him between bar and
car. In fact, I found myself in a respectful, appreciative
mood in our initial talk. Throughout that night he was,
behind the dark glasses and the Southern gentleman's
drawl, seethingly honest. Although the joviality of spirit I
had witnessed during his lunch earlier never surrendered
completely to the prevailing mood of his conversation, it
was obvious that he was in pain. The preface of his aptly
titled book of short plays, *Dragon Country,* did not need to
be embellished upon any further. Dragon Country was the
country of pain. An uninhabitable country which is inhabited.

As we spoke through the long hours of the night, he
would punctuate anecdotage with sudden glimpses of glar-
ing insight, or rather the anecdotes more or less set the
stage for the revelation which would come at last, perfectly
timed. I became aware that this was a kind of test. He was
past looking for a warm body. He was looking for a warm
mind.

Pushing through the accumulated curtains of the tropical life on this island, it became clear that theatre was still

alive and well in Key West, albeit it was sitting in a teetering chair in a swamp of other people's stale alcohol.

In that syncophantage to the famous is a certain betrayal of self. I was ready to abort this acquaintance if it became apparent that this was the price of admission to his company. It had been the tendered price in the past during my life in publishing and the one time I tried it I didn't like it. But that fear could lay at rest for Tennessee was far from needing or wanting that ploy. What he did require was the test of honesty. I countered his litany of universal opprobrium with my own remark: "If your image is so distasteful to you, why did you enhance it with those stream-of-consciousness comments you call your *Memoirs?*"

"You're right about those *Memoirs*, baby. I wrote them at a low ebb, as I presume is apparent from the pages themselves. But my publishers knew that scandal sells and I knew that my own personal scandal was imminently beyond that of those whom I rather randomly exposed. I could justify that book only because I was so honest about myself. I call for a new morality in the book, although few understood my meaning. People are so ready to condemn their own humanness. My life was an open book already, my agent advised me, so why not make some money? It sold very well. But I think I'm right in saying I never saw a cent from it. The publisher retained the right to the cash, you might say. Or International Creative Management, if they were on the scene yet. At last, after I complained and bitched until they wouldn't have it any more they made me an offer. They would pay one dollar per autographed copy. That's the only money I made on the book. They'd send down cartons of them and I'd spend an hour or two each day, after my writing, autographing them and then we'd send them back up to Manhattan."

The rewards of greatness were obviously far removed

from my own imagining of them. Here was Tennessee, the
world's greatest living playwright, reduced to earning an
income from autographing books.

"Did you make much that way?" I asked.

"Now that you ask, I wonder. Jim, do you know if we
ever received a check on that matter?" Jim Adams was a
cousin from Eastern Tennessee and seemed a bright, ebullient, bountiful person. A painter, he had accepted Tennessee's invitation to come paint in Key West with room,
board, and a small income in exchange for his services as a
driver and casual helpmate.

Jim smiled brightly and laughed. "It's a mystery to me.
But, Tom, the way you guard your mail I never know much
of anything unless you tell me." He said this warmly, but
the observation was there.

"Since Cousin Jim would seem to prefer that the matter
remain in the dark, we'd better check up. Jim, on Monday
morning we're calling Mr. Eastman to determine this."

Applying my own inner logic and experience to this
revelation and exchange, I found it difficult to believe that
a major publisher of a major writer would find means of
withholding all royalties and that they would then treat the
writer with such contempt that they would pocket Tennessee's autographing fees as well. Or had he truly bankrupted
even the established business customs of the country?

But Tennessee had a compelling gift. As he weaved
through his stories—perhaps it was the timbre of his
voice—a kind of truth would always emerge. His plays and
stories revealed emotional truth, often metaphorically, and
it was more than likely that his speech—what I came to
know as his "living theatre"—would as well.

Admitting that there might well be grounds for some of
the charges against his character with which Tennessee had
begun his talk to me, one seemed truly insupportable:

illiteracy. Ironically, this seemed to be the most unlikely charge to be based on truth and yet Tennessee's perceptions were to a degree contagious and I wished to pursue his grounds for this contention.

"Can the New York Times accuse a major contributor to twentieth century literature of being illiterate?" I asked.

"You didn't know that the New York Times knew all, baby? That, if in their insufficiency of research and information they elaborated on what they think or wish to know, when they print it it becomes true. They say I have no cultural reference points in my plays. That I am unread and that my plays and stories reflect this."

"But Tennessee, what forms do these charges take? I don't read the New York Times with any regularity, but I do know their format. Are these essays in the Sunday theatre pages? On the Op-Ed page? Just how do they get this nastiness about you across?"

"They practice the art of pervasiveness. Pervasiveness of attitude. It's just all strung out between the lines. They don't want me to go down as America's greatest playwright. They want Eugene O'Neill. They prefer him because he wasn't queer. You've got a lot to learn, baby, a lot to learn."

"Are the nation's morals then set in a kind of star chamber at the New York Times? Do Mr. Sulzberger and his staff have weekly meetings to determine what everyone in the United States should think?" I asked.

"There's no necessity for a star chamber. Their mind's made up. Their mind's been made up since the 60's. They want me to stop. But I've got a few surprises for them left in me."

In my first hours of knowing Tennessee, I was astonished at these revelations. Obviously, in these upper reaches of accomplishment things were done differently. Initially, my

reaction was to discount these observations and put them
down to the late night and the influence of alcohol. But
then I was caught up in Tennessee's own inner logic. These
things didn't seem so absolutely impossible. I determined
to keep my reservations, but not allow them to color what I
heard.

"If I may ask, what are you working on now?" I said, in
order to move the gist of the conversation along in a more
positive direction.

Looking around the bar at the attentive revelers with a
baleful expression of some paranoia, he said, "Let's keep
that to ourselves, shall we? Jim, shall we invite Bruce over
to Duncan Street for a nightcap and a swim?"

"Sure, after all, you've known him a couple of hours now.
I don't think he'll murder us in our sleep."

"Good. Let's get going. I'm tiring of this environment,
you know."

I had begun to pick up on the humor-laden paranoia
which seemed to inform much of Tennessee's passing re-
marks. In deference to this approach, I said, "Surely we
won't dare walk to your car unescorted? We've all read of
the nearly tragic mugging you and Dotson Raider received
right here on Duval. Those redneck youths might be waiting for you."

This was in reference to an event which had recently
gone out on the wire services, quoting the writer Dotson
Raider on the details.

"Of that particular 'shot heard round the world,'" said
Tennessee, "I can only say, politely, that that particular
event never happened."

Jim Adams brought around the little white Honda,
which he described as their "Key West limousine." On the
short ride to 1431 Duncan, Tennessee gently put his hand
in mine. "Don't worry, baby. We're friends and friends

should offer simple comfort to each other when they can. Often I find it's better than talking. Why do people who know each other well think they always have to chatter to one another? What comfort and ease there can be in one another's presence, that's the ticket!"

Arriving at Tennessee's home, it was pleasant to see with what simplicity he lived. The house was not only unpretentious, it was downright undecorated and simple. You entered the living room and viewed the kitchen described with such ire in Tennessee's *Memoirs*. On the right was a bedroom, at this moment with a bed barren of its clothes. Books, mostly paperbacks, were scattered about. The one famous object in the room was the wicker peacock chair, in which Tennessee had often been photographed in recent years.

The steamy Key West night had made me long for the late-night swim that Tennessee had promised. "Shall we swim?" I asked.

The pool looked wonderful, under the palms which clicked in the warm night air, their leaves black against the lighted cerulean blue of the pool.

"This is my life now," said Tennessee. "I swim twice a day. I write over there [a small, white outbuilding] in the mornings. Have a swim. Lunch if I feel up to it. Rest. Perhaps another swim. Then dinner and into the night."

"Between injections of morphine, of course," I said. He laughed.

The night. I was to learn that the night was the ultimate challenge of each of Tennessee's days. How just to get through them. Here he still employed state-of-the-art pharmacology to carve his way to dawn.

He wandered from the pool into the house where he remained for some time. I dressed and followed him in, thinking perhaps he had retired in the Key West manner,

unceremoniously. But he was up and about, going through
the kitchen cabinets. He turned to me and said, "I had
thought to provide you with a nightcap, but I've forbidden
hard liquor in the house. I'm looking for some wine."

"Don't," I said. "It's late and I have to fly back to
Chicago tomorrow on an early flight."

"Oh, don't go, baby," he said. "Stay a few more days.
Perhaps I'll go back with you. Check it out, you might
say."

"I'd love to stay, Tennessee, but really, I can't. I'm afraid
I met you on the last leg of this trip."

Tennessee seemed not to have heard me as he went to a
closet and brought out a stack of bed linen. He proceeded
to the downstairs bedroom and began to make the bed.
There was much fluttering of white as the diminutive
figure tried to fit the sheets to the bed.

"Please don't bother, Tennessee. If I stay, I can make the
bed myself."

He turned to me with his wry grin. "I just didn't want
you to say that I couldn't offer you proper sleeping accommodations," he said.

I had begun going through some of his paperbacks and
picked up a frayed copy of Hemingway's Nick Adams
stories.

"What you got there, baby?"

"Hemingway."

"Now there's a *literate* writer," he said with a chuckle.

Since Tennessee sensed that I really was determined on
going, he sat down and began to talk. These late night,
"after the ball is over" sessions became a regular feature of
our times together. They were easily the richest of times.

Tennessee sat there thoughtfully stroking his beard,
looking at me.

"What's up?" I asked.

"Let me fill you in, if you would oblige me. When I said

I might come on to Chicago with you, I wasn't just whis-
tlin' Dixie, you know. Chicago's always been my kind of
town, review-wise. You're taking your life in your hands
going from this climate to that, of course. But it might fit
in with my current occupation to check out the scene as it
is at this time."

"As I said, what's up?"

"You seem to be someone who'd know about Scott and
Zelda. Do you know much about her?"

Save Me the Waltz, Zelda Fitzgerald's book, had recently
come out as had a biography devoted more or less to her. I
said I had read these books and that I had found Zelda to be
talented and an individual of great personal tragedy. I did
not subscribe to the popular notion that, perhaps, after all,
she was the real genius of the family, however.

"Well, baby, that's what I've written about in my new
play. It's *Clothes for a Summer Hotel.* It's my first full-length
play in a long time. I think it contains some of my best
writing. I met their daughter, you know. Kept trying to
look her in the eye. To see if her parents were there, you
know. Perhaps they were, perhaps they were."

"She's a writer, too, I understand. I haven't read her."

"I have not read her. From what I've heard, it's not my
kind of thing, you know. But she'd seen a play or two of
mine, yet had nothing much to say. A pregnant and silent
commentary," he said.

"Perhaps she was shy."

"I told her I was writing a play about her parents. I
gather she rather hoped that that wasn't true," he said.

"I'd love to read it."

"Oh, you'll see it soon enough, if you're so inclined. I'm
still working on it. First we go to the Kennedy Center in
Washington, D.C. Then, if we survive, we're taking it on
to Chicago. Do you know Miss Cassidy?"

"Miss Cassidy is a great favorite of mine. She does a

weekly commentary on the arts on our cultural radio station, WFMT. I grew up in her neighborhood and I have met her a few times."

"Is she well? And her husband? I had heard he was quite ill. It saddened me to hear it."

"To my knowledge, he's still here. I haven't heard otherwise."

"Gerry will be in *Clothes*," he mused. "She's probably too old for the earlier Zelda. They say her voice is going. Can you see her as Zelda?"

"I've always loved Geraldine Page. Ever since I saw her in Truman Capote's *A Christmas Memory.* Sook, I think. And she was wonderful back in the 60's in *Summer and Smoke.*"

"That was a long time ago," he said. "Much water has passed over the dam, so to speak. But people love her. She'll be good for the play."

"José's directing *Clothes.* José Quintero. He got through to Gerry. She told him she'd do the part if he directed it. Doesn't say much for me as a playwright, does it?"

"Who's Scott?"

"If it's who I think it is, I may as well stay right here. You know, when you tune out on occasion, as you may say I have, certain august personages in the theatre world tend to discount your views. My own agents think I've lost my mind. The Audrey Wood incident. International Creative Management. Milton Goldman. Busy little Mitch."

Except for Audrey Wood, whose presence lingered on from Tennessee's *Memoirs,* I had heard nothing of the others, but at this point Tennessee did not wish to elaborate.

"I've seen broadsides and posters all over the island announcing Tennessee Williams Week, or a festival, or both. What is all that about?" I asked.

"In the fullness of time, I have come to be considered the major tourist attraction in Key West. They seem to have forgotten about the nice weather. Or the fishing. So the Chamber of Commerce and some theatre folk put together this idea, on which, in a weak moment, I placed my blessing. But it's a horror for me. Tourists pick up these postcards which have a photograph of the house. It has the address. They wander over for a peek. I have either to flee the island or hide. It's a technicality, but since I endorsed the idea, I should, in some sense, be around. I've taken to swimming in the gulf. I can do that with a becoming sense of anonymity. No one expects me to be out there for some reason. When I'm home, Jim has his orders: Keep them out or back he goes," he chuckled.

Jim had vanished into the night after he had let us off at the Duncan Street house. "The hunt is evidently on," laughed Tennessee as Jim had pulled off in his Key West limousine.

"*Clothes,* you know, is a surprise for everyone. It's my first full-length play since *Night of the Iguana,* and no one thought I'd ever write another. I can pretty much vouch for that. But I've been taking care of business and myself, and here in Key West I've found some peace. I don't imagine I have long to go, but I still have things I want to say. I know they wish I'd stop. That I'd just quit and leave the field. Nothing is more irritating than having a playwright around who's clinically alive but by all rights should be dead. Dead I'd be more use to them. They could do what they like. But that's not going to happen yet."

"But they, whoever they are, must want your new work. Someone must be producing it. Quintero is directing it. Geraldine Page is starring in it. It would seem there's enthusiasm somewhere along the line," I said.

"Enthusiasm? Now there's a word I particularly like in

this context. Dread is almost certainly the more appropriate term. You know, I'm very involved in seeing a new play
of mine through production. In short, I'm around. When I
first dropped a note to Mitch Douglas that the new play
was coming along, communications from New York con-
veyed the notion that of course I would rather stay on here
in Key West or go to Sicily or the Orient. How it must have
tickled them to think that I'd be dead drunk in Tokyo
while they fiddled with my play on Broadway. Put whomever they liked in it. Edited the dialog. Spread the word
about that this was a heroic effort on their part in honor of
the befuddled and dishonored writer. Yes, baby, dread is
certainly the most appropriate term. 'Almost' just won't do
it. Now that they know I'm sticking around, it's dread,
pure and simple."

This intimate and behind-the-scenes view of getting a
new play on the stage was quite an eye-opener to someone
who had only seen the finished product upon the boards.
And, I could sense that Tennessee was enjoying opening
this new vista to someone innocent of professional theatre
life. His delivery of this narration was punctuated and
enlivened by his frequent Southern chuckles.

"You're in for a lot of work," I said.

"You know, when radio and TV interviewers, when they
aren't making hay on themes of alcohol and drug addiction—most recently, you know, morphine addiction—
think to ask me what a creative writer is made of that
differentiates him from others, I don't go into elaborate
theories on the subject; but I have determined an answer I
like to give them. And that's that an artist has an excess of
energy. It sounds rather dull and these interviewers of
whom I spoke almost certainly attribute this rather lame
analysis to a lifetime of drug abuse, but I sincerely mean it.
Through the years it just seems that I have more energy

than most. So, you're right, baby, a lot of work it will be. But as groggy as I may sometimes be or seem to be, I've still got a lot of the old energy. And I'm keeping it up. Swimming, resting, and confining my intake of alcoholic beverages to red wine. This is taken in small quantities at lunch and then, admittedly, through dinner and sometimes on into the night. But I feel I can handle it. I'm at my typewriter at six A.M. and I work for at least three hours each day."

It was time to go. As he waved me to the bed I would never use, Tennessee said, "I always send very generous bouquets of red roses to my lady stars along with the obligatory telegram telling them to break a leg on opening night. But this time—and I envision them huddled together in those cramped dressing rooms—they'll get a variation on the theme. My little note will say, 'Don't anyone pull a knife!' Yes, that should do it," he chuckled.

As I wandered from his little white house down Duncan to Duval, I pondered the powerful project on which Tennessee had embarked. It saddened me that the genesis of *Clothes for a Summer Hotel* was his seeming need to prove some kind of literacy beyond his own work. The media and its movers had worked persuasively in his mind. He now seemed a kind of aesthetic athlete gone back into training for a comeback. That I would be there to see it all was a thought far from my mind.

CHAPTER II

***

Page by Page

SHE WAS DRESSED APPROPRIATELY for an actress in a state of siege. Geraldine Page entered the Bagatelle Room of Maxim's de Paris for the February 26, 1980, opening night party for *Clothes for a Summer Hotel* in Army/Navy surplus raiment. Her pea coat and blue knit cap still sparkled from the severe snow which was fulfilling February's promise to Chicago.

Too, she had arrived late. Having failed to kill the party, by conspiring with the p.r. people to tear the invitation from the backstage bulletin board, she had had to change her plans. But this late entrance upped her status immeasurably and protectively. Against the Belle Epoque mirrors, her shabbiness and the no-longer-strictured gray hair assumed a kind of mythic imagery. Mistakenly, the feminists among the guests assumed the gesture was for them and their sisters. Now, at sixty, virtually everything she did was symbolic.

Geraldine was in the early stages of revolt. *Clothes for a Summer Hotel* had been entered into under auspices differing from those which developed since she had signed. Among her backstage cohorts she was often less than discreet about her plans and how they were coming undone.

José Quintero, who was directing the play, had promised her Tennessee as a silent partner. The play, as originally upon the boards, was imperfect, yet surprisingly much better than any theatre observers had expected. The shape *Clothes* was in was really no worse than many of Tennessee Williams's earlier full-length plays. It was part of his creative process to work on them as he saw them acted out.

Many of his most memorable lines and scenes had been conceived and written on the back of envelopes or on the margins of playbills. Later, they would be properly typed and given to the director.

The play that Geraldine Page had seen before signing was a one-woman show: Zelda Fitzgerald in her last stages of disintegration with flashbacks to earlier and happier days. This aspect had been the strongest in the early phases of the play's evolution, but now there were causes for alarm. For her, the production at the Kennedy Center in Washington, D.C., had gone well. Tennessee had played to type. Newspaper accounts told of drunken arrivals at cast parties, no-shows for interviews, the accustomed litany which had entwined and almost sunk Tennessee's ability as a viable and supporting force for the successful production of the play. While Geraldine Page was not so pleased as she might have been had he never left the confines of Key West, his behavior in Washington was serving her purpose. She would be both star and savior of the production. The ball was firmly in her court.

The preparations for the Chicago run had begun with calls from Tennessee in Key West. After I had left the island, we had talked off and on. Then Washington. Then silence. Then a brisk call from Tennessee who wanted to set the Chicago stage for some productive action of his own.

I had hired a car and driver to pick him up. He arrived accompanied by Jim Adams. I could see we were in for a new scene. Tennessee had dressed for the midwestern winter. Capturing two media images at one swoop, he wore a Yves St. Laurent exercise suit and was bundled against the cold in a coyote parka. For effect, the hood was always pulled up, exposing only a portion of a hirsute visage and those fiercely gleaming eyes. So, attired for ongoing exercise and appropriate coverage from the elements, Tennessee made his Chicago entrance.

As the car pulled onto the expressway, he began to tell me what was to come. It was immediately apparent that I had to be provided with some background so that I might aid him effectively in his plans. "Baby, you may as well know that I've got spies all over. One of them virtually sits at *her* right hand." "Her?" I asked.

"Gerry has lost not only her voice but any inhibitions she may once have had. I've heard that she's worried to death that I'm in fairly good condition. She tells her friends that the play just isn't quite right, you know. That any showing of huge and loyal audiences will be for her and not the play. She already named her target. It seems we're in for a Tony for Gerry and a closing for me. But this is just between us."

Somehow all this didn't fit into my preconceived notions of Ms. Page as Sook. She must be a truly tremendous actress to so cleverly put into the shade her true identity. This was a remake of *All About Eve,* but the star was after the playwright! I suggested my feelings to Tennessee.

"You'll see for yourself one night. I intend for you to get to know Gerry. She won't make it easy but we'll get it done, baby, we'll get it done."

The next day, a Sunday, I had a reception for Tennessee at my home in Old Town. I invited a large number of my friends in the press as well as friends who were politicians. It was quite a group, but I wanted Tennessee to make important new friends fast. He was in fine fettle. Drinking moderately, dressed in the blue Yves St. Laurent jumpsuit, he regaled the group with glittering tales of the show business world. Tales of Tallulah, Vivien Leigh, Elizabeth Taylor, Paul Newman. He put on a brilliant performance with every vignette timed to the minute. When, after several hours, it came time to bring the curtain down, he rose in a courtly manner and began singing in a discreet but audible voice, "The Party's Over." The whole warm, friendly, eye-opening event was chronicled by reporters from the *Chicago Sun-Times,* the *Chicago Tribune,* and even *Time.* The ripple effects lasted throughout the Chicago run of *Clothes for a Summer Hotel.* Both Tennessee and I were confident that he was now on a much firmer footing than could have been imagined a matter of hours before.

The Monday morning papers brought the good news that America's greatest living playwright was in Chicago to oversee the production of his newest play and that he was a warm, friendly, engaging, and totally unpretentious Southern gentleman. This jibed with my experience, and I was pleased that we had served up so potent an antidote to the poisonous print that had come before.

At the first dress rehearsal which I attended with Tennessee at the Blackstone Theatre, I could see where Gerry was taking the play and how much help she had been given by whomever had cast the production. After all, though *Clothes for a Summer Hotel* would present new material on Zelda and help celebrate her as a potent feminine American type, there was Scott to be considered.

Tennessee nudged me in our box above the stage as

Gerry made her entrance offstage. I had just heard the celebrated Page swoop as Zelda screamed for her "Bach fugue." "Just watch her now, baby," he whispered. "She's under the mistaken impression that she'll have the stage to herself as she plays Zelda from her rather post-menopausal ballet studies to death by fire. Nothing will stop her." A quiet cackle.

As alarming as was the image of Geraldine Page practicing at the bar, even more alarming was that of Scott Fitzgerald. How had it happened that a black-haired British actor came to play a very blond-haired American writer? "Kenneth Haigh, you know," said Tennessee. I didn't know. The performance was perfunctory and absolutely uninformed as to the character of F. Scott Fitzgerald. Haigh played him like a Formica vanity salesman.

As we watched the emerging sadness on the stage, Tennessee would make comments and notes. One note was most memorable. The note he handed me to read said: "José, make him wear a blond wig or fire him!" This incident signalled the commencement of Tennessee's actively aggressive phase of bringing *Clothes* back under his control.

There could be no doubt that he was right about Haigh. The man was probably a capable actor, but he had been sadly miscast and he seemed to perform by rote. His presence on the stage exuded discontent and misunderstanding. That he had been cast in the first place was beyond imagining.

It was decided that this night would be a propitious evening for dinner with Gerry. To this point, she had made no attempt to speak with him and Tennessee thought that a little reconnoitering was in order. With all the irony of "theatricality," as I was coming to know it, we chose a restaurant called Paradise Cafe. It was not at all convenient to either Tennessee's or Gerry's hotels and was a good distance from my home. But Tennessee had ascertained that what he needed was some time in a taxi. It's difficult to get out of one once it's moving.

Halfway to Paradise Cafe there was a furtive ruffling through the coyote parka, a patting of pockets, and a concerned expression. "My pancreatic enzymes! I must have left them at the hotel. Driver, would you be so kind as to return to the Blackstone Hotel?"

When we reached the hotel I offered to plough through the snow to get his enzymes, but Tennessee was insistent. Bundling himself against the pelting snow he moved with amazing grace into the hotel.

Geraldine Page and I were alone. To help make her more approachable, I reverted to her incarnation as Sook. "I really loved the Truman Capote films. You were wonderful."

"It was almost impossible to get them made. We got a last minute grant and were able to go ahead." Thus, she dispelled the glamor of those productions.

There was a silence and then a very firm, "Now look. I don't know who you are, but I know Tennessee's up to something. You tell him not to call Rip. The play's going to be fine. By the time we're on Broadway it will all work out."

"I don't know who Tennessee calls. I see him only occasionally during rehearsals and then either at lunch or dinner," I said.

Of course, I knew that the call for Rip Torn had already gone out. Haigh had refused the blond wig and a replacement for an actor to play Scott Fitzgerald was first on Tennessee's agenda. As a matter of fact, a call was in to Rip Torn in New York where we had left a quantity of numbers where Tennessee might be reached that night. Among them was the number for our destination, Paradise Cafe.

To Tennessee, Rip Torn seemed a natural for Scott Fitzgerald. Beyond his appropriate coloration, his persona would fit the role like a glove. Somewhat ravaged, highly intelligent, neurotically sensitive. Without a word, Rip could convey these qualities by just walking out onto the stage. But he had one decided and seemingly insurmountable drawback. He was Ms. Page's husband.

The minutes ticked by as we waited for Tennessee, and the tension in the cab became palpable. It was impossible for either one of us to be consoled by the image of Ms. Page as Sook.

"Would you call this some kind of wonderful biochemical resurrection, or what?" Gerry asked. "He's been scrambling his brains for decades with all those pills and things and now he's acting like it's 1958 again."

"My memories of Tennessee don't go back nearly so far," I said. "I only met him six weeks ago. He just seems to want some companionship during this opening ordeal and I'm happy to oblige. I'm very fond of him."

Gerry was restive. Her gray wool mittens were used to defog the cab window as she searched for Tennessee's figure through the deepening snow. "What's he doing these days? Exercising? I don't think he's drinking so much. His speech isn't so slurred as it was. And he's at all the rehearsals making those goddamned notes. What he's done to poor Kenneth!"

"You two having a good time, Chicago-style?" chuckled Tennessee as he entered the cab. He held the pint-sized bottle of pancreatic enzymes in his hand and brandished it to demonstrate the fruits of his labors. "I'm back in business," he said.

When we reached the restaurant we were, of course, late for our reservation but the table had been saved for us. As well, a sheaf of messages were thrust into my hand. "Read them to me, baby," said Tennessee.

"Rip Torn's called for you three times. Here's the number. Also, a call from Mitch Douglas of International Creative Management," I said. I handed Tennessee the messages.

"Oh, if Rip's been calling, I just better call back right now," offered Ms. Page. "It might be the children. I'll excuse myself and call Rip. Why don't you just give Mitch a call, too."

"The messages are for me, to all indications," said Tennessee. "Let's order our meals. We've kept these people waiting long enough." Whenever Tennessee spoke with authority it would have taken a General Patton to ignore it. It was just such a tone that he used now.

Gerry had gone quite silent. She perused the menu in the guise of Alma Winemiller in *Summer and Smoke*. Put upon, slightly mad, obviously repressed. Tennessee said, "It will be hamburger and red wine for me, baby. Not to insult the ingenuity of the menu since the owners of this establishment are clearly your friends. But pure protein is what I need. Pure protein." The fact that we had spent over an hour and travelled a considerable distance for fare we could have had in the hotel restaurant was not overlooked by Ms. Page. She sighed and ordered some fish and salad.

A protean silence hung over the table as the owner of the restaurant approached. "A call for Mr. Williams. Rip Torn."

Upon hearing her husband's name, Gerry rose instinctively. "It's for me," said Tennessee as he was led to the phone. Left alone with Ms. Page, I filled the minutes by discussing the menu with her. Food trends, nouvelle ideas. "Oh," she said, "I suppose they do have to think about things like that."

Tennessee returned. "The children are fine," he said. "Rip will attempt to reach you at the hotel later."

"Bruce has been explaining the menu to me in your absence," said Ms. Page.

"I've found Bruce such a thoughtful friend," said Tennessee. "I wonder if Haigh is going to wear that blond wig or not?"

"Oh, you know very well he'll never consent to that," said Ms. Page with some exasperation. Dinner chatter reverted to talk of the weather and little else.

My welcoming party for Tennessee was paying off. His reputation as a dependable guest and charming conversationalist had brought forth batches of invitations. Tennessee submitted them all to me. "I don't want to make any mistakes now," he said. "Please tell me if you know any of these people and if they're suitable. I want to conserve my energies for the play."

When Tennessee had first called me from Key West to advise me of his trip to Chicago, he had set some ground rules for himself, among which was a very firm one of limited access for the gay community. I knew this had to be handled judiciously since much of his playgoing market was gay. Because of his undisguised reputation, I was somewhat surprised. "I'm coming up there to work," he said. "No gay restaurants or bars." When I told him that his opening night party was planned for Maxim's, he said, "That's the ticket. Everyone knows that's not a gay restaurant."

On occasion, however, ambitious emissaries of the gay community would wait for him at his hotel door or backstage of the theatre. One of the most irritating incidents occurred when he had to cut short an interview with WFMT's Studs Terkel because someone from *Gaylife,* a Chicago special market paper, ate into his time on his way to a meeting with Studs. It wasn't the fact of the matter that irritated us both, but that the interview hadn't been scheduled professionally.

At this time there loomed the production of the operatic
version of *Summer and Smoke* by the Chicago Opera Company. Members of their board could not be ignored or
snubbed socially. I urged Tennessee to accept the invitation
from one board member, which he reluctantly did. It was
about midnight Saturday when I received a plaintive call
from him. "Get me away from this uptown shit," he said.
"Jim, tell Bruce where we are so we can get out of here."
Jim Adams got on the phone. "I don't know whether it's
the guest list or the clear acrylic baby grand that's upset
him most. Are we far from you?" He gave me the address
and I arranged to pick them up. Tennessee got back on the
phone. "Please come here as quickly as you can. I can only
tell these people what lovely teeth they have a certain
number of times."

A much better party was given the next night by the
octogenarian dance legend, Ruth Page. It was to prove the
opulent setting for our denouement with Geraldine Page.
The party was a celebration of Ruth Page's recently published book of memoirs, *Page by Page.*

We had to come to the party along Lake Shore Drive. It
was dusk and the powdery white snow falling through the
blue dusk and against the gray skyline was lovely. Tennessee was in a subdued but engaging mood. As we drove
along I pointed out certain landmarks to him. Nearing Ms.
Page's apartment building I indicated the Carlyle highrise,
the residence of columnist and Chicago's nationally-known
show business arbiter Irv Kupcinet and his wife, Essee. His
interview with Kup on WBBM-TV was yet to come, but
Tennessee was familiar with the journalist and referred to
the tragic death of their daughter many years before. "Did
they ever find out who murdered her?" he asked. "It's
another unsolved Hollywood crime," I said. "But you see,"
he said, "it's simple. Essee did it!" The sibilant s's lasted

through my reaction to the outrageousness of the comment. We both laughed cathartically about the very notion. He applied his sense of play to everything. The tragic was never immune.

When we arrived at Ruth Page's, the New York City Ballet Company had already arrived and was posed elegantly about the teak-floored, expansively white-walled apartment. Ruth Page, whose voice is a bubbling brook of light and sparkle, welcomed us effusively and positioned us at a corner table with a view.

It was truly a lovely and memorable evening. As we talked with Ruth Page, who politely remembered all of Tennessee's work and commented intelligently upon it, we had the pleasure of viewing the elegance of the assembled group of dancers, their profiles positioned against the rampant de Koonigs.

As we were just falling into an unaccustomed state of the ether of relaxation there was a tight bit of confusion at the door. A waiter had opened it to admit a guest. It was Gerry, once again attired in her now familiar battle garb of pea coat and knit blue cap. She had been moving fast, because the snow still sparkled in the antennae of her hair.

She made a beeline for our table. Acknowledging Tennessee with only a grimace, she addressed herself to me. I rose. With her hands still clothed in her gray woolen mittens she began pounding me on the chest. The ballet company turned its collective head in our direction, en pointe.

"It's nothing," Tennessee said pleasantly. "Gerry just doesn't want us to know what a fine actor her husband is. Who knows, we might even put him in a play!"

CHAPTER III

In the Bar of a Tokyo Hotel

"WE'RE GOING TO HAVE to keep our health up if today is any indication. They're packing pistols, baby. They're packing pistols," Tennessee said idly as he unpacked the bag of groceries we had purchased for the evening meal. Earlier, before the great adventure with our first televised promotion for the premiere of *Clothes,* he had advised, "It'll be linguini with white clam sauce tonight, baby. And I'll make it. It's healthier my way than that restaurant fare you seem to be so fond of." Here was another scene from the imaginary "Domestic Williams" which I had formed in my mind to accept anecdotes of his home-like nature. Tennessee Williams puttering about the kitchen. We were at my home in Old Town and Tennessee shooed cousin Jim and me out of his culinary arena. "Get to know each other," he said. "I'll let you know when dinner's ready."

Accordingly, we did. I thought I'd regale Jim with the tale of our visit to the studios of WBBM and Irv Kupcinet.

"It was quite a scene, Jim, as Tennessee fully meant it to be. He arrived bundled in his Siberian manner, the coyote parka wrapped so about his head that just a tuft of beard and a gleaming eye emerged to greet the somewhat astounded staff of Channel 2. We were ushered with nervous ceremony into the vacant office of a staffer since there was no green room."

"Did Tennessee know where he was?" Jim inquired.

"Knew where he was and playing it to the hilt. Kup, as Irv Kupcinet is known, arrived shortly after and couldn't resist putting me down as I didn't form part of his own personalized 'media mafia.' He said 'I see you're in the hands of the world-famous Bruce Smith, Tennessee. Good to see you. Essee sends her love.' "

"How often do you suppose Essee had actually seen Tennessee in the past in order to qualify as someone who could send her love to Tennessee?" Jim inquired, blissfully ignorant of the wiles of show biz.

"In all of time, perhaps ten minutes. But she means well. But then her husband did an astonishing thing."

"He put his tongue in Tom's ear," laughed Jim.

"Something even more astonishing. He brought out a bottle of wine. You should have seen Tennessee's expression. It was priceless, imploring me to go along with this as calmly as possible. Kup left the office for a corkscrew. Tennessee said, 'Do you suppose he's trying to get me all liquored up before I go on the air?' Of course he was mirthful in this surmise, but the occasion did give us pause. I told Tennessee that I thought Kup was just trying to be one of the boys."

"A situation fraught with possibilities," laughed Jim.

"Well, Kup came back with the corkscrew but couldn't seem to open the bottle with it. Perhaps he's unfamiliar with such things. In any event, he handed me the bottle and asked me to see what I could do. We then played loving cup and passed the bottle around for a swig each."

"You mean Kup actually took a swig, too?"

"He did. And I never liked him more for doing it."

"Chicago sure is a frontier town," said Jim.

"Well, you can say that we don't stand on ceremony, at least in powerful places. After we each had our swig, Tennessee gleefully observed that this had been a very pleasant interlude, but did Kup have anything further in mind? Kup harrumphed and checked his notes. Shortly, a crew member came for them and they moved onto the set."

"Well, I saw that part of it," said Jim. "I thought he was very amusing sitting there with his parka pulled up around his ears."

Tennessee, who was listening from the kitchen, said, "They didn't get it, baby. They just didn't get it. I thought I was being amusing about the weather conditions here in Chicago, but they thought I was too far gone to take off my fur. I knew that bit of business with the fur would keep the camera on me. Did it, Jim?"

"The camera didn't move from you, Tom," said Jim.

"Our friend Kup didn't have too much to say about the play," Tennessee called from the kitchen.

"Tennessee, doesn't it bother you that all Kup talked about was your past problems with alcohol?" I asked.

"It only makes me thirsty, baby."

I told Jim about our post-performance trip to the supermarket for our dinner supplies that night. A feature editor of one of the major city papers was standing in line at the checkout counter. He had been at the party for Tennessee at my home and called out a greeting. Tennessee waved back in a rather careless manner, having forgotten the person. The editor told the person next in line that that was Tennessee Williams. "Why would anyone name someone

for Tennessee Williams?" she asked. Nonplussed, the editor replied that this indeed was the real Tennessee Williams. "Are you certain?" she said. "Tennessee Williams
shopping and sober in a Chicago supermarket?" Tennessee's
reputation had preceded him.

Jim and I would occasionally turn to watch Tennessee
through the kitchen pass-through. Admittedly, it was
slightly disorienting to have this playwright in your home
slicing tomatoes for his special Italian salad. He looked
much like some of my elderly, caterer friends in Manhattan.

"We'll make this dinner in memory of Frankie," he said.

"You better know what you're getting into if Tom's
thinking about Frank Merlo," said Jim.

This was the first time Tennessee had mentioned Frank
since being in Chicago and he thought he'd make the
reference clear. "This was a meal that was a favorite of
Frankie's and mine," he said. "Our happiest times were in
Italy together. When we had good Italian food back in the
States, it was a celebration for us."

Jim lowered his voice. "Tennessee goes on about the
tragedy of having lost Frank Merlo," he said, "but he was
rotten to him, even at the end. He was always out in bars
while Frank was dying in the hospital. He'd bring him an
occasional meal from one of their favorite Italian places,
which, of course, Frank couldn't eat, but the gesture made
Tom feel he was taking care of Frankie as best he could.
Frank was the best thing that ever happened to Tennessee.
He was the most long-suffering person I've ever met. I
think that his unhappiness with Tom was what killed him.
He tried so hard and received so little."

If that were true, the Frank Merlo who emerged in
posthumous conversation with Tennessee was someone approaching sainthood. In the short time that I had known

Tennessee it seemed to me clear that he could successfully deal with his own emotions only on paper. This is no very unusual indictment for a creative writer.

That Tennessee had now begun an elaborate kind of courtship of me had moved from mild surmise to some certainty. I do not mean a romantic courtship in the usual meaning of that term. I mean that it was becoming clear that Tennessee was seeking someone rather actively to fulfill the role of companion. His invitations to me in that regard were touching in both their subtlety and ingenuity.

He had begun the practice of taking copies of his works from my library shelves and autographing them for me, inscribing messages which had to be pondered and even researched in order for them to yield their true meaning. For example, the day before he had left my copy of his book of short plays *Dragon Country* on the coffee table newly inscribed: "To Bruce: 'I Can't Imagine Tomorrow' Love, Tennessee." The inference was that I should read the play to determine the real meaning of his message. Of course, I did this. The play deals with people who more or less existentially merge as housemates without any real discussion as to the formalities of the arrangement. It's a sad little play and its message touched me. It turned out to be the muted overture to his program of having me move to Key West and take over the management of his sundry enterprises. That someone should come in and responsibly fulfill this role was beyond dispute. I was touched and flattered as this invitation was slowly revealed to me in the days ahead. But I knew enough of Tennessee's emotional history than to be seriously tempted by it. My alternative was to offer him my friendship. Not by blatant word, of course, but by deed. Tennessee had made the mode of our communications clear. Of course, I felt I had made a good start in that direction already.

Tennessee's repast was quite good. We were rather thoughtfully spooling our pasta, when Tennessee looked up and said, "Why don't you come on down to Key West when we finish here?"

"I wouldn't mind taking a break from this weather, Tennessee. What a nice invitation." In this manner I could accept his goodwill, yet diffuse any implied inquiry into permanence.

"We may have to flee town, you know. Unless Claudia Cassidy comes through. We can't count on the other notices. And Claudia didn't like *Iguana* too much, either, so we may not be entirely safe even with her."

"You stay with Tom long enough, you'll learn all about fleeing," Jim chuckled.

We let the matter rest. Tennessee took his nap by the fire while Jim and I cleared the dinner. Tennessee wished to be awakened in an hour so that he might explore some of Chicago's non-"uptown shit" style of nightlife.

It was during these after-dinner naptimes that other aspects of Tennessee's life would resurrect themselves. This evening he awoke from his nap to request a pen and paper. "I dreamt about Kip," he said. "I have a poem in mind in memory of him. I want to write it down." Kip was a lover of more than thirty years before. With the poem written that night, he began one of his last plays, *The Silver Victrola*. It chronicled his affair with this beautiful Canadian dancer, who had later decided that the gay lifestyle was not for him and had deserted Tennessee for a young woman whom he married. Although Kip escaped the full emotional ramifications of an affair with Tennessee, he, too, died from cancer, as had Frank.

Having committed the poem to paper, Tennessee was ready for a little exploration of Chicago nightlife. Accordingly, we bundled against the snow and settled into a bar ramble. Glancing around at the all-male clientele of the bar he had chosen, he reverted to his remark of earlier that evening. "Bars are the emblems of woman's failure, at least in America," he said as he ordered a glass of red wine. "At least all the women in my life have seen their role as of the maternal order. To keep me from the cup, you might say."

"And your brother Dakin?" I queried, familiar with the St. Louis incident where he had institutionalized Tennessee against his will.

"Yes, in this regard I have to place Dakin among the women in my life, just as I placed Tallulah among the men, you know." He chuckled. "I often said that Tallulah was the greatest man I ever met. She was a great drinker and, despite her reputation, had no real interest in sex. Humor and booze were the great staples of her life."

"Then she wasn't the great lesbian of lore?" I questioned.

"All those ladies of a certain period played around with each other on occasion. It was just part of their education. Men remained their real interest. But Tallulah was one of the truly great actresses until liquor came along and affected her judgment. At one point, which effectively estranged us, she thought she should appear in a revival of *Streetcar*. She was so old at the time that the notion was absurd. And so I told her. She insisted that her approach would be totally original. That she understood the Southern psyche much better than Jessica Tandy. Her's would be the sole authentic performance of this role. No, I told her, let's not go into it. Just no. I had no wish to insult her but the occasion made it unavoidable and that was the end of that. Another bad ending."

"Other than Frank's portrait, Vivien Leigh seems to have been given pride of place in your gallery. Was she as lovely as she seemed?"

"Vivien Leigh was the most profoundly lovely actress

and woman I ever knew. And, she was a warm, generous person. She had no idea she was so ill the last time we met, but I could tell she hadn't long. I'm glad she went fast. Her film role as Blanche was all her own and quite genuine. But I liked her work in *The Roman Spring of Mrs. Stone* which is the only film version of anything I wrote that I truly admire. It just worked."

It was clear that Tennessee was not ignoring the scene before him, aware of "all the sad young men" drinking away any opportunity for love and even more casual adventure.

"I hate gay social life," he said suddenly. "I'm glad you're not into it. I always felt I was under some kind of curse, you know, being homosexual yet hating the lifestyle, or, at least, most of it. I won't say I haven't done my share of camping. Frank hated that side of me. He should have stuck around. I let it go years ago. I think men are so aesthetically beautiful. Now, all I really want is to stroke smooth, young skin. The purely sexual is pretty much over now. I can't stand to bring my old body into a scene with anyone I find attractive. I'm a realist. Why would anyone want to go to bed with me? Except for what Jim here calls starfuckers. There's a great, descriptive term.

"I've never taken advantage of my position in the theatre world to secure what are so romantically called sexual favors. For one thing, actors don't interest me as people. They're pretty much an immature, self-centered lot and I've found it's better to avoid them on a personal level."

One of Tennessee's favorite tales was of the young Warren Beatty. As yet relatively unknown, he was up for the role of the gigolo in *The Roman Spring of Mrs. Stone*. The star was Vivien Leigh. After a satisfactory reading in a Los Angeles hotel, Tennessee gave the young Warren Beatty the part. Later, wandering the hall to his room, Tennessee found himself accompanied by Mr. Beatty to his hotel room door. Tennessee said good night, opened his door and began to enter. Beatty began to enter with him. Tennessee closed the door on him and said, politely, "You've got the part, baby. You've got the part."

It would be natural to see this anecdote as gratuitous, but it was told completely without malice. I think it amused Tennessee to add these few strokes to the public rendering of the image of Warren Beatty as super-stud, but he did not do it in any way to diminish Beatty. In a very real way I'm sure he thought it only added to the actor's humanity.

It is true, however, that Tennessee had no very high regard for the acting profession, except for the true exceptions he always took care to mention: Laurette Taylor, Vivien Leigh, Jessica Tandy. Among men, he almost never singled out an example for great acting with the notable exception of Brando. He did, however, have comments to make on those actors whom he thought were a little less than earth-shattering in their roles. One who came under benign criticism was Paul Newman. "Newman is so slow to learn," he would say. "By the time he had his lines, whatever emotional force that was generated by the other actors in the scene would have been dispelled."

I tempered my interpretation of Tennessee's Paul Newman anecdote with my knowledge of his great unhappiness with the production of the film version of *Cat on a Hot Tin Roof* on the whole. He was always going on about the repression of the Hayes Office, which extended the sexual hypocrisy of the nation into filmmaking. In the film of *Cat*, homosexuality is only implied, which makes many of Brick's ravings and ragings largely inexplicable. "As Newman was forced to play him," he said, "you'd think the whole point was that he was an irrational alcoholic who happened to have some bad luck during a drunken jumping exercise."

"I've rewritten *Cat* full force, you might say," he would often say. "There should be no doubt now as to what the play's about. So many of my plays have been made into so many bad films that it's a wonder I have any reputation left at all.

"Newman was so extraordinarily good-looking, you know? Not my type, but unforgettable," he said as he looked about the bar, his eyes occasionally lighting on a particularly arresting figure. "Chicago doesn't have to take a backseat to anywhere as far as its men are concerned," he said warmly. "They're a good-looking lot."

It was on this night that he passed along my favorite of all his theatrical anecdotes to me.

"You know about the first lady of the American theatre, baby? Miss Helen Hayes? Well, I have it on the ultimate authority that she can't act! I knew that all along, of course. But the ultimate authority on the subject is, of course, Miss Hayes herself. She admitted it to me one day when we met in the Gotham Book Mart in New York. She couldn't avoid me with any sense of decency, so we began to chat. We hadn't seen much of each other since the debacle of the London production of *Menagerie,* which was a miserable flop. After some carefully edited catching-up, she said to me, in a rather brisk manner I thought, considering the content of the remark, 'I know I can't act, Tennessee. You may put yourself at rest on the matter. I own up to the matter freely.' And, with that, she left the bookstore."

CHAPTER IV

―――――⟿―――――

Exit Libris

THESE WERE THE DAYS of wine and snow. Each day of work: writing, rehearsals, discussions, ended with dinner at some quiet spot; quiet discussions at my fireside and then a cab ride back to the Blackstone Hotel. Tennessee seldom left my home without a care package of several bottles of cabernet. The first night of this pattern, Tennessee had found his request for a corkscrew beyond the resources of the Blackstone, so he had requisitioned one from me. Typifying his mannerliness of this period was the call from the manager of the Blackstone the next morning asking me what arrangements he could make for the return of the corkscrew. I advised that he might consider the corkscrew on permanent loan to Mr. Williams.

Our nights by the fireside hatched many plans for the expansion of both the man and his work into new media. For example, he had made no recent recordings of any of his works. It occurred to us that recordings of portions of his greatest works might offer the definitive readings of the text. No other important playwright had been offered this technological benefit and, given that Tennessee did feel himself to be something of an actor and certainly an intimate of the text, recording readings seemed invaluable for the theatre of the future. As always, however, Tennessee could raise a macabre lantern to these suggestions. "The morgue at the *New York Times* has got my obituary ready to go, baby. No reason we shouldn't record at the earliest opportunity. I'll be checking out soon." "Checking out" was currently his favorite euphemism for "passing on to his reward."

On these nights before the fire, as Tennessee held sway, garnet glass in hand, it occurred to me what an extraordinary chance it would be for a university to create seminars with Tennessee discoursing on the twentieth century theatre in just this fashion. Happily, he responded quite positively to the idea. "Do you think you could arrange a little academic showcase for me here in Chicago, baby?" he asked. "I think if once I got a good rep for these things I might have the chance of doing them more often. I'm not considered reliable enough just now to expect anything in the way of an invitation. But maybe with some inside help we could pull off a seminar or two. I love to work with serious students of the theatre and with young writers."

The University of Chicago seemed the natural stage for this event. They were contacted but were unused to the idea of programming an event of this magnitude within the time frame we gave them: one week. Accordingly, I used my family contacts at the Newberry Library, the repository of the manuscripts of many major midwestern writers, to set up a seminar of reading there. There, the spirit of the humanities proved more prompt. A reading with a question-and-answer period to follow was programmed for a week ahead.

To catch Tennessee in the mood was the caveat of the times. Any negotiations which dragged on in the usual manner of business would never be consummated. In this I had my position. The tradeoff for a quicker pace was Tennessee's stature as a writer. Most often, however, persons and organizations held to the prevailing view that Tennessee was no exception to the rule.

A few days before the scheduled reading, the library advised that the reading was a complete sellout. "I divine a sense of destiny in this," said Tennessee. "When your godfather was the director of Newberry, he let you read Edgar Allen Poe late at night in the stacks. It seems only fitting that you return the favor by tendering this other relic of the old South to the present management."

This would be the first public reading by Tennessee Williams in more than a decade. It marked another important stage in his personal reclamation of self. And a second happily occurred as well. The reading would be taped by Chicago's cultural radio station, WFMT. This would prove to be the only recording made of Tennessee reading his works as he had come to interpret them in his last years. The reading is extraordinary. And it still haunts whenever it is replayed, as it often is, on WFMT.

Through the unstinting generosity of Nancy Goldberg, owner of Maxim's de Paris, we would make Maxim's our home before any event of public importance. A lunch or dinner within its pristine Belle Epoque environs always gladdened the soul. "I've been checking out the decor while I've been waiting here for you," said Tennessee as I arrived for the lunch which was to precede the Newberry reading. "This is really some place!" he added. That was the highest praise he ever proffered a commercial establishment in my experience.

I had arrived to find Tennessee and Jim Adams ensconced in Maxim's equivalent of Booth One. Tennessee

had abrogated his usual red wine in favor of what looked
suspiciously like a double martini on the rocks, with two
olives. Jim, noticing my awareness, volunteered that this
was the second of what would be a notable series of liba-
tions. And Tennessee was fidgeting. On the table before
him was a generic brown prescription medication bottle. I
thought I recognized it as the pancreatic enzyme store from
the night of the Geraldine Page episode. Presently, Tennessee picked it up in a casual fashion and began to regard it in
a studied manner of appraisal followed by a lingering
glance. "It's empty, you know. Did one of your critics steal
into my room and run off with this life-giving sustenance?"
In this way, Tennessee amusingly betrayed his worry about
critical response to his new play. The reviews, not the
pancreatic enzymes, were the "life-sustaining sustenance."

In any event, the bottle was empty and something
would have to be done. "Jim knows I can't live without the
pancreatic enzymes," he said with a look of humorous
paranoia at Jim. "Does anyone know where I could get a
refill, without any great hazard to life or limb?" I asked, "Is
the prescription bootleg or legitimate?" "I don't know the
professional status of my Key West doctor on a daily basis,
but I do believe he still has his license to practice," he said.
I huddled with a Maxim's waiter, who obligingly set off
through the snow to get a refill for his luncheon guest.
Errands for Tennessee were always conducted with a sense
of great urgency, fueled by his constant assertion that he
was "checking out" in the near future.

Though Tennessee had dressed rather nattily for the
opening night party, he had now returned to his casual
attire mode. The Yves St. Laurent jogging suit had been
put back into service for the afternoon's reading. It would
acquire legendary status in the course of the afternoon at
the library. "What have you picked for the afternoon's

program, Tennessee?" I inquired. He did not speak, but, both hands grasped about his martini, he peered at it avidly. Jim thought he'd save the day. "Tom thought he'd read from his books of poetry, *Androgyne, Mon Amour,* and *In the Winter of Cities.*" Tennessee raised his head. "I'm going to read Hart Crane," he announced. "I must read from Hart Crane. My reading will be a selection of his verse and my own." "Will you recite from memory, Tennessee?" I inquired. "I need the text, baby. I wouldn't trust to my memory just now."

Lunch was as simple as could be had at Maxim's. My anxiety about the reading was mounting rapidly. I wondered if the reading would proceed in a desultory fashion, as the martinis were not having a very salient effect on Tennessee. I tried to shadow my irritation, but Jim picked up on it. "Do you have the texts?" I asked. Jim smiled. "Would Tom have the texts?" he asked. "Then I'll have to get them from home," I said rising to go. "Please keep Tennessee here until I get back," I said to Jim.

The situation was idiotic. I had to speed in a cab through the snows to retrieve books for a reading that wasn't half an hour away. I tried to soothe myself with notions of the prerogatives of genius. This proved a limited palliative.

When I returned to Maxim's with the books, Tennessee was in quite a mellow mood. He had ordered a Sambuca Romana with three coffee beans "for luck" and presumably in memory of the good days in Italy with Frank. Although well-fortified, he wasn't drunk and he seemed to have brightened considerably in comparison with his earlier demeanor. In true show business tradition, he had revived for the reading.

Though advance publicity on the reading had secured an attendance never before witnessed within the staid Romanesque fortifications of the Newberry, our reception provided problematical. The grand staircase to the reading room was six deep on either side. We quickly realized a side elevator was the only way up. Before we could turn from the stairs, an anonymous greeting from a stalwart of the stacks set the continuing tone of the day. "How dare he appear at Newberry dressed like that?" the aged hippie shrieked at Tennessee. A theatrical shudder from the guest of honor sufficed for response as we secured the safety of the elevator and rose to find whatever greeting might await us.

Our procession to the sanctum sanctorum of the director's office was not simplified by the hoards of eager fans. The scene was Fellini-esque. But from this dreamlike multitude we emerged into the hard daylight of our official reception at the library. Not experienced enough at this time to know that blatant bad behavior was almost inevitable when Tennessee made an appearance, I was especially unhappy to find that no official reception had been planned for Tennessee. Inexplicable, in that the director was an associate of our family and had been instrumental in setting up the reading at such short notice. Evidently, he had felt that providing the fiat for the occasion was sufficient. He had delegated the balance of the program to his staff, with largely unhappy results.

Instead of the civilized greeting which would have been in the traditional manner of library-sponsored occasions, we found the director's office tabled with radio interviewers. Perfectly nice interviewers, but absolutely not appropriate to the mood of the main event, Tennessee himself. But the smart slap of winter had revived Tennessee and had put him in a rather brisk and obliging mood. Somehow he obliged the interviewers, but the oasis of quiet civilization which I had promised Tennessee was absent.

A delegate had been sent to see that Tennessee actually

got to the rostrum, but that was the extent of the hospitality offered.

Somehow it had escaped the notice of the management that the sole reason Tennessee was at Newberry was because of my own association with the library. I had told him of the importance of the library to my own, youthful education when Stanley Pargellis was director of the library. As my spiritual godfather, he had given me free reign of the stacks once the library was closed at night to the public. This seemed a romantic notion to Tennessee, who believed always that it was the spontaneous exception to systems that allowed the human spirit to grow. I had provided Tennessee with an image of an island of culture and quiet. But now we were again surrounded by sharks and mavens with no host to close the great oak doors upon the unhappy scene.

Though the librarian proved an inexplicable no-show, there was a glass case in his office which offered some symbols of solace to us. Somehow, the library had come into possession of some mementoes from the estate of Charles Dickens. Before us was a signet ring, the writer's inkwell and pen. The ring particularly interested Tennessee. In the play now being produced, *Clothes for a Summer Hotel,* there is an evocative moment when Zelda throws her wedding ring into the wings, disparaging this "covenant with the past." "But just such a covenant with the past has saved us now," said Tennessee. "But, baby, are you sure we're in the right library? I'm sure this situation isn't what either of us would have anticipated."

And well he might have wondered. And yet, like Dickens's ring, this moment would help consolidate our friendship. Tennessee was familiar with the unkindness of those known to us. He grabbed my hand in sympathy. "I'll give them a reading they won't soon forget, baby. Then we'll get out of here. The only answer is to flee from the silly unthoughtfulness of others. Do you know a back way out of here?"

The night before, as we had discussed his reading at the library, Tennessee had advanced the notion that another of his projects which I might help him undertake was to find a suitable repository for his papers. Harvard and Yale were likely candidates, as was the University of Texas at Austin. However, the romantic evocations of my memories of Newberry had moved him. As of the night before, Newberry was a leading candidate for the papers. To support the notion, I had mentioned the library's extensive collection of American writers' manuscripts, among them those of Sherwood Anderson and Ben Hecht. I had done my bit to return the Newberry favor. Tennessee was right. You could count more on the kindness of strangers.

With elaborate high-tech pageantry, radio station WFMT was setting up its recording equipment as we entered the reading room. It was standing room only. Mixed in the crowd to our right as we entered was yet another occasion for us to flee. Tennessee nudged me. "There's Dakin and his wife, Joyce. I won't talk to them. He'll probably try to get up on the stage with me in order to advance his campaign for the U.S. Senate." Dakin's political ambitions were the stuff of dementia.

I could sense that Tennessee now held the experience before him as an adventure. Where his work was concerned he would not slough off, no matter how contrary the conditions. I handed him the three books from which he would read. "Sit where I can see you, baby. I'll read to you as if by the fire at home." He was then caught up by the staff and brought to the podium.

That reading, as captured by WFMT, is a Proustian madeleine. To hear it as it is replayed by that station is to have the whole Newberry experience brought back in its totality. How once in those hallowed halls, etc.

The media yahoos, the critical curious, the few serious fans now formed a scene more Nathaniel West than Fellini. They were at last subdued. And the reading began.

Tennessee's reading of Hart Crane's *My Grandmother's Love Letters* at last silenced the last boob in the house. It was a murmured cry from the soul. Even the most dense were not immune to the combined psychic thrust of Tennessee Williams and Hart Crane.

The generous reading was over. Tennessee signalled me from his stand. The library group, expecting some further dialog with the poet and perhaps an autograph or two, would find that a cold shoulder could be returned. We moved with dreamlike purpose through the assembled crowd, shuddered away from the waving Dakin, found the elevator of our escape. We were out into the blissful snow and cold air again. We paused to breathe. "Where to, Tennessee? I think I've selected enough destinations for one day." "To the nearest bar," he said. "And the darker and sleazier the better."

And, as we settled in the cab, he added, "We may thank God that that is over." He took my hand. A kinder part of the day could now begin.

CHAPTER V

―――――――― ❧ ――――――――

Ghosts

FOR TENNESSEE, THE WOLF at the door was always the day ahead. And so, he was ruthless in his determination to secure the earlier part of the day for his own self-preservation. The formula was set. Write from dawn until ten or so. Swim. Dress for the day ahead.

As opening night for *Clothes* drew close, this pattern was secured through the intervention of his friends. No one was to importune him before noon. Lunch would signal a return to the world at large, when the ritual hamburger would be consumed with a few associates in a favored restaurant. There, the subject of his discourse was scarcely a happy one. In his new play, he had chosen subjects and subject matter so reflective of his own state of mind that *Clothes,* as it evolved, became a kind of diary. As we would talk during our lunches, he would often note sudden thoughts on the restaurant napkins, which would then be handed with some urgency to the director or stage manager during the afternoon's rehearsal.

In a way which could not be ignored, Tennessee was addressing his entire mythic self in his new play, moving through Zelda—a fragmented and unrealized Blanche du Bois—to Scott, whose persona seemed to Tennessee close to his own. Certainly, the parallels were patent. The self-destructive, alcoholic behavior of Scott Fitzgerald, considered in tandem with his traumatic difficulties in extricating himself from the mutually-destructive relationship with his wife, elicited parallels that were obvious to those close to him. In this consideration, Zelda became a dynamic symbol for Blanche and the other troubled women of Tennessee's plays. It seemed that, in this last phase of his career, Tennessee was himself trying to extricate himself from the coils of the women of his past, both in his literature and in his real life. Certainly, there were obvious parallels with his sister Rose, who, lobotomized for schizophrenia, had been hospitalized in an asylum for close to half a century. His mother, Edwina, was now in her last year and still exerted a psychologically draining hold on him. She would emerge in discussion as the play wore on. According to the ethos of the play, Zelda was fated, not only to never realize her creative potential, but to die by (purifying?) fire in her asylum of residence.

But this ongoing rite of purification or self-analysis, if such it was, was about to hit a brick wall. And, in true Tennessee tradition, the wall was of Tennessee's own making.

Purification certainly seemed the order of the day as Tennessee pursued his daily program of exercise, sensible diet, and limited intake of alcohol (save for exceptional circumstances). The clarifications taking place in his behavior seemed to be working themselves out as the destinies of Zelda and Scott worked themselves out in *Clothes*. He was far from the inebriated writer, and the theatre world was having a hard time getting used to that fact.

For Tennessee, there was no socializing with the players downtown at the hotel. If he were ignored, they seemed to think, perhaps he would go away. Little of his input, albeit on napkin notes, was implemented within the play. Scott, as interpreted by Kenneth Haigh, "purveyed the grace of a cigar store Indian," according to Tennessee. And Tennessee continued to work for his removal from the cast.

At rehearsal one Saturday afternoon, shortly before opening, we sat together in his box. The box offered an encompassing view of the stage. In the opening scene of the play, where Haigh entered as Scott with his pathetic attempt to gain entrance to the asylum which held Zelda, two nuns, envisaged as devouring, threatening birds of prey, guard the entrance to the asylum implacably.

"Visually, an interesting scene," said Tennessee. "But there's Haigh again. He won't wear the blond wig. He won't say the lines with any appropriate cadence. He's going to do more to ruin the play than Gerry. If his part doesn't make sense, they may as well bring the curtain down now."

Tennessee pronounced the name Haigh with such precise savagery that its association in his mind with the word hate could not be missed. Haigh and hate were taking their toll on the play.

On this occasion, two new observers had been brought to the scene. Gary Tucker was a former Chicago minor league director of offbeat productions; his offerings, *Whores of Babylon* and *Turds in Hell,* had run out of support in Chicago sometime before. Tucker had then moved on to Atlanta, where he had directed two well-received short plays by Tennessee, *A Perfect Analysis Given by a Parrot* and *The Frosted Glass Coffin.* Tennessee had gone to Atlanta to see these seldom-produced later plays and had liked what he had seen. In the box before us now were Gary

Tucker and his friend, Schuyler Wyatt, a beautiful blond young man.

Sadly, Tennessee felt at this time that Tucker had a sincere vocation with him in advancing the acceptance of his much underplayed later plays, most of which had been published in the compendium entitled *Dragon Country.* With the advent of these two we had moved even further into that uninhabitable land.

Gary Tucker had swung into the theatre world on the braids of *Hair,* for it was that liberating production that brought open sexuality more honestly to the stage. It had spawned a new age in theatre and Tucker was among its heirs. Going by the sobriquet of "II"—a reference to his renowned physical endowment—Tucker was a marginally outrageous theatre presence. His personality and production history was precisely wrong for the new direction of Tennessee's life and theatre.

Tucker wished to capitalize on the decadence of Tennessee's late work and his much publicized life. He thought only to aggrandize himself through association with the Williams name and to put himself forward as the admirable "savior" of whatever was salvageable of Tennessee's late work. For his purposes, it was imperative that Tennessee remain as comatose as possible. And Tucker brought just the sex and drug kit necessary to effect his control.

At this moment, that Saturday afternoon in the box at the Blackstone, these revelations, while guessed at, were yet to be confirmed.

Tennessee had not warned me that we were to be joined by these two members of his personal cast. But he loved to pull surprises like this one out of the blue, as cousin Jim had advised me. A degree of psychological sadism was operative and he loved to see the abrasive clash of the

sensitive with the brashly opportunistic. It was his ongoing way of punishing the world and everyone in it for the
injustices imposed on him, whether real or imagined. My
mode of defense in this matter was to switch from my role
of friend—which had now been betrayed by the advent of
the people in the box—to that of writer. There was this
duality in my relationship to Tennessee. And it was he who
had advised me to take it on. While the friend would try to
abort transient treacheries, the writer would have the solace
of writing it all down.

I now pondered the situation in the box that was being
woven with consummate skill while the production of
Clothes unravelled on the stage below. Schuyler Wyatt was
an example of male beauty tailor-made for Tennessee's fond-
est fantasy. This was so true that he could scarcely keep his
eyes on the work of the stage as he stared at Gary Tucker's
protege. While this situation might make good copy, I
could not forgive Tennessee for joining so viciously in so
obvious a set-up.

The kind of drama that the purveyor of sleaze from
Atlanta was creating with the help of his anchorite was not
one I had come to see. And so I left Tennessee in his box
with his new friends. As I left the theatre, I wondered just
how bad the situation would become. If Tennessee now fell
in with Tucker's people, he would merely confirm the first
suspicions of many that Tennessee was acting irresponsibly,
self-indulgently, and, ultimately, self-destructively.

At that time, the underworld into which Tucker was
leading the willing playwright was ordered by civilization's
reverse image of drugs and disease. As the architect of my
own life, my structures were conceived in an upward manner, toward the light. I hated what might be happening
now to my hopes for the "new Tennessee" who had introduced himself with so much hope just a few months ago on

that bright day in Key West. At that sad moment, Tennessee had joined the risen ghosts of Scott and Zelda. He was venturing towards the void.

"You didn't take to my new friends," Tennessee said to me in his first call to me after this last revelatory rehearsal.

"It's not my world, Tennessee. I can't work in it. It's entirely foreign. I can't relate to it. It's why that part of the gay world has such a hideous reputation. And, because it's the most visible part of the gay world, it holds the entire minority back from gaining any real acceptance as a responsible social entity."

I had planned my position carefully, because Tennessee, while knowing where I stood, had to be told that I knew as well.

Tennessee continued, "Schuy's a very beautiful, sensitive person. An actor, a painter, a singer. Gary's going to make him a star. When we all go back to Key West I'm going to paint him." If his acrylics were aquiver, I knew we were in trouble. He only painted those he loved. And his last portrait had been of Robert Carroll, according to Jim.

I hadn't seen Tennessee in several days. "What will you do now, Tennessee? Can you fix the play before it gets to Broadway? I heard the preview audience loved it. You could get rid of Haigh if you concerted your efforts. You have the legal right to do so."

"I'm too tired right now, baby. I'm hoping a little skillful rewriting will compensate for some of, shall we say, weakness we now have." It occurred to me that Gary Tucker, wishing to advance his career in the theatre, would not wish a reputation as an upstart and so undoubtedly encouraged Tennessee to self-defeating convention. Tennessee would now have an even more difficult time getting a good play on Broadway. He had found and welcomed in the enemy's fifth column.

"You mean you haven't settled anything with Rip? A

COSTLY PERFORMANCES   77

powerful performer would seize the role and make it powerful enough to act as a foil to Gerry's madwoman. You've
done the groundwork. Surely you could get this much done
by the time of the New York opening."

"Gary doesn't seem to think that's as important as we
do, baby. He seems to bring a fresh perspective to the play.
Maybe we've just seen it too often."

"So now you're taking your cues from Gary Tucker,
Tennessee?"

"He has some experience you know. He did so well with
the Atlanta productions. I see him as a kind of director
without portfolio, though I'll keep that information from
him as long as I can."

Gary Tucker had now begun his Machiavellian reign. It
would effectively see Tennessee through to the end of his
involvement with play production and insure the failure of
all his dramatic ventures.

Gary was a creature of the theatre world. Seeming to
wish for Tennessee's success and to be sympathetic to his
plight in old age, he was, of course and in fact only
attempting to advance his own career. Importantly, he
knew that there was a theatre life for him after Tennessee.
His career could advance as he continued to control Tennessee and the production of his plays through to the end. For
these purposes, a new, healthy Tennessee was a true stum-
bling block.

At this point in the progress of my association with
Tennessee it could be but bitter suspicion, but it did seem
that Nemesis had sounded the first ring of her reign. And,
in truth, henceforward, Tennessee didn't stand a chance in
hell of being anything important in the theatre world
again.

But for now we kept such cold counsel to ourselves. We
would struggle forward to try to save the day. After all, an
opening night was at hand.

CHAPTER VI

Where's the Bach Fugue?

THE PHONE RANG BRIGHTLY at eight on the morning the play was to open. It was cousin Jim calling for Tennessee. "Tom's up and about and wants to be sure you're with us tonight at the theatre."

"Are we going to be joined by the Atlanta hustlers? Or will this be a relatively civilized evening?" I inquired.

"Tom seems to be avoiding them just now. I think your absence made him think a little. If you could just be objective about this, you could see just how funny and true to form this is. Tom loves games. He knew you'd react with all the horror you have. Now that he's had his response he wants to put it all behind us for a while."

"For a while? Do you mean he plans to pull out this little bag of tricks again? You know I don't need this kind of thing. I won't have anything to do with it."

"Please go along with him for now. You've been so good for him and remember how crazy he gets before an open-

ing. He keeps asking for you, but he thinks you'll scream
at him if he comes to the phone personally, and he's not up
to it.

"Come on. Let's have a nice lunch and then meet for
the theatre later. Tom wants to take a swim after lunch,
which should calm his nerves a bit. Tom keeps going on
about the party tonight. You just have to be with us in
our box."

The party at Maxim's was in the offing and I didn't
particularly want to jeopardize that. I met them for lunch.

Tennessee was hesitant and defensive at first, but then,
after a glass of red wine, he relaxed and began to discuss the
play which was to open that night.

"As you know, I long ago discovered that Ken Haigh was
no actor for my plays, but now I've lost the female lead as
well, it would seem. Gerry has lost her voice. She says it's
temporary, what she calls her Chicago voice."

He held out little hope for the reviews. "Only Claudia
Cassidy will be kind. The others can't wait to draw blood,"
he chuckled rather sorrowfully over his red wine. "But
whether Claudia will be kind enough to save the play
remains to be seen. I don't trust much in anything these
days."

Our meeting for pre-opening drinks was called for at the
Illinois Athletic Club, which Dakin called home when in
Chicago. It had an Olympic swimming pool and he let his
brother use it. The club was only a block from the Blackstone so we could walk there easily.

Grimly, the sepia visages of past IAC officers stared
down at our table.

"Aren't you amused to find yourself among this pervasive
corporate mentality? How suitable for the night's adventure," I said.

"They do all look a bit like Dakin, don't they? And

Dakin looks much like our father, which may partially account for my dislike of him. Of course, Dakin doesn't drink like our father. Those particular genes were handed directly to me," he said with his frequent punctuating chuckle.

An aged barman approached our table. "Get my friend here his J & B. He's the nervous type." Indeed, Tennessee had become apparently calm. He was perfunctory and businesslike.

"Jim, once the curtain's rung down, we're fleeing this city," he said suddenly, reversing my impression.

"I think we'll just go to Bruce's cast party instead, Tom," said Jim. "Don't be silly, Tom. This isn't going to be a bad opening."

That afternoon I had spoken with Claudia Cassidy, upon whom Tennessee reposed his faint hope for a critical success. "I never come to cast parties," she said. "But tell Tennessee that I send my best love and my good wishes. I hope he's well. I hope for the best for the play."

I passed on this greeting to Tennessee, who warmed in response. "Claudia is so wonderful and kind. She gave me my start in a fashion, you know, with *Menagerie* here in Chicago in '44. We almost never meet personally, but I still feel close to her."

Folly upon folly greeted us upon arrival at the Blackstone Theatre. First, Chicago's media concierge (Henry Fonda's term), Margie Korshak, denied that she had any tickets for the playwright and his guests. Obviously peeved that she wasn't quite Tennessee's cup of tea, she thought she'd do what she could to upset the apple cart. Tennessee simply called the theatre manager and we were ushered to his box.

"I assume that's p.r., Chicago-style," Tennessee laughed.

"Aaron Gold, the Chicago *Tribune* columnist called this

morning to inform me that she was in a snit and that we'd
better watch out," I said.

"Watch out for a p.r. person like that? In any event, she
tried but failed to keep us out of the theatre on my own
opening night," said Tennessee.

The curtain rose as the stiff-legged Ken Haigh paced
before the gates to the asylum. The overly familiar lines
were not improved by their wooden delivery. But what
we all were waiting for was Gerry's entrance. Could we
hear her?

Gerry's first line came from backstage. "Where the fuck's
my Bach fugue," swooped the Page voice as Zelda Fitzgerald. Fans everywhere in the audience applauded her.

"That will get her through the first act, I would guess,"
Tennessee chuckled warmly. That was about it for Gerry in
this role. When she actually appeared on the stage it was at
once apparent that it would take a great leap of imagination to accept her as interesting as she practiced at the bar
in her ballet attire. Later, when she was to frolic on the
beach with her illicit love, the French aviator, even her
most fervid fans rattled their programs.

"She's aged so," whispered Tennessee. "I wonder if all
this exercise is all too much for her. Can she possibly save
the play like this, at least until I get a new Scott?"

As the curtain rang down, there was a respectable response from the audience. But no curtain call for Gerry.
Perhaps now, no Tony for Gerry. The three of us went
backstage to congratulate Geraldine. Passing the cast notice board, I noticed that the invitation to the night's party
had been torn away. I pointed this out to Tennessee. If he
had seemed too preoccupied to care at this moment, I
would have forgiven him, but he was as outraged as I.

"I think that's more p.r., Chicago-style," said Tennessee.
"Your friend in the lobby is hell-bent on her mission to

upset us, it would seem." Poking his head into each of the dressing rooms, he said to each cast member, "My friend here and his friends have gone to a lot of trouble to have a party for us tonight. Presumably, a lady last seen in the lobby of this theatre managed to get back here to remove the invitation from the notice board. The party is at Maxim's on Astor Street. We hope to see you there." We never did determine whether it was Margie Korshak or Geraldine Page who had tried to sabotage the party.

Tennessee's engaging act of kindness did much to repair the damage done by the Atlanta contingent. By the time we arrived at Maxim's, the Bagatelle Room was already well on the way to being filled with Chicago's glitterati. We had the local Rockefeller heiress, who needed to belt back a few in order to summon the Dutch courage necessary to meet the playwright. A further scattering of socialites and the usual writers and editors. Our hostess, Nancy Goldberg, seemed to move above it all and yet her presence insured that the socialite segment behaved itself. She was, after all, the social godmother to them all and had had the opportunity of rapping quite a few knuckles in the course of her career. As for the press, only one achieved a slight stir.

Henry Hanson, a reformed political writer from downstate Illinois and who now reigned as the pundit of the art/theatre/society nexus in Chicago, had thought to bring Dakin, his good friend. Dakin and Henry seized the opportunity to buttonhole Tennessee in an attempt to fuel the flagging embers of Dakin's phantasmagoric political career. They had one-track minds in the matter and Tennessee was dismayed. He didn't need this on his opening night.

After the two had dispersed, Tennessee said, "Dakin just keeps hammering away at these simple ideas of his. He has

no political career. And it's people like Henry, rather un-
kindly I think, who keep revving up his fevered brain. But
I have come to expect the worst from Dakin for a long time
now. You see, Mother dropped him on his head when he
was three."

CHAPTER VII

On the Wings of a Dirge

"THEY'RE LINING UP FOR blocks eight deep for *Sugar Babies,* baby, and I'm bringing on a dirge! You tell me what the prospects are!" mused Tennessee in his call to me from his home in Key West. The *Chicago Sun Times* drama critic, Glenna Syse, had described *Clothes* as a "haunting lyrical dirge." Tennessee admitted he liked the description of his work as haunting and lyrical. "But dirge, baby? A little too close to the bone for someone like me, who's about to check out."

Shortly after the Chicago opening, which was a moderate success and which made money for its producers in Chicago, Tennessee followed his dictum and fled to Key West. He sounded rested and sane when he called me to invite me to join him in New York for the Broadway opening of *Clothes.*

"New York has never been my favorite place, as you know. Would you do me the courtesy of joining me there to see what we might achieve with the Broadway production?"

The delivery of this March 21, 1980, invitation was in the manner of the overly courteous Southern gentleman, a role which Tennessee would assume when faced with a problematical situation. It served him well. It was impossible to refuse him.

"My travel agent is awaiting your pleasure as to the flight you wish to choose. She will have a fine first-class seat waiting for you."

This was a new development. Tennessee had never paid for anything except for an occasional hamburger. His stay in Chicago had been almost entirely on me.

One upshot of his Key West musings seemed to be a role reversal in so far as the host position was concerned. If I had picked up the tab in Chicago, he would do so in New York. His manner of conveying this was in his best theatrical tradition. Greeting me at the door to his Manhattan apartment, he embraced me dramatically, one clenched fist full of fifty-dollar bills. "Money isn't going to be our problem in New York, baby. This town may have a lot up its sleeve, but if money can help, we've got it." If he was trusting to the power of the buck, which he did wind up doing, then he was in the right town.

This fistful-of-dollars moment was to prove emblematic. The world-as-theatre mode was now in high gear. His Manhattan apartment, which he despised because of its aseptic horrors, was softened by a random selection of extravagant theatrical mementoes. On one wall of the living room was a theatrical rogue's gallery, with autographed portraits of Vivien Leigh, Jessica Tandy, Maureen Stapleton, and Tallulah Bankhead. As a handsome punctuation point to this collection, at the end of the row of pictures, was a photograph of Frank Merlo, Tennessee's late lover and good friend. He had been dead more than fifteen years, but his calm, understanding, and handsome face reflected a warm spirit back into the room.

As clipped and professional as a concierge, Tennessee led me through the apartment, pointing out its amenities. "You, of course, will have the bedroom to yourself," he said, in a bemused manner, as though that matter were high on my list of concerns. "And I will get what sleep I can here," he said gesturing to a daybed by the window. His rest/work area was a dramatic set design in and by itself. He had set up his large easel between his desk and bed. A paint-bespattered dropcloth was flung over the easel. This effected a room divider for him. "I like to be near my work," he said, by way of explanation.

"Are you painting, Tennessee?"

"I'm pretty much alone here, you know. I turn to it after I've completed my daily writing. I don't like to go out of doors alone here. Now that you're with me, we have a lot to do."

His writing table, on the other side of the easel from the bed, was an existential salad, manuscripts tossed about with some pieces of clothing—socks, mostly—paint rags, and empty wine bottles.

"Have you done any more work on *Clothes,* Tennessee?"

"For better or for worse, baby, that is more or less concluded for our present purposes."

"What, then?"

"A new play. It's important for me to have a new play in work before the notices are in for the one in production. I always fear that if I'm knocked out by the reviews, I won't have the courage to write again. This is my insurance policy. To start a new play, you know."

"A work of historical personages, like *Clothes?*"

"Not again. It's about the richest woman in the world.

I've titled it *Masks Outrageous and Obscure,* which is a line from Sara Teasdale. I have Vanessa Redgrave in mind for the role."

"You seem to rise in some haste from your labors," I said, gesturing to the chaos upon the writing table.

"What's that, baby?" He seemed unaware or at least unconcerned about the swirl of typescripts and handwritten notes, some of them wine-stained and many torn or crumpled.

"Now that you're here, let's have a fashionably late dinner. I've been waiting on you. There's a little place nearby that I like."

"Where's Jim these days, Tennessee?" I asked.

"As of now, he's residing at my home in Key West. The tourists visit such terrorism on us that someone must occupy my property at all times."

"Finding an unpopular restaurant with good food in Manhattan is almost impossible," Tennessee observed, cryptically. "But this little spot where we'll go is a little off the map. I don't think we'll be besieged there or otherwise inconvenienced."

As we left for dinner, Tennessee issued a litany of distaste for the building in which he had his New York apartment.

"This is a truly ghastly place, its nearest cousin of the Russian gulag. True, Manhattan's a rage of social horrors, but the security here is unbalanced. You need a plastic photo i.d. card just to get through the front door. I'll have to get one of these damned things for you, so that you can come and go freely." He sighed with disgust and displeasure at the system.

Wrapped now in his signature coyote parka, to which costume he had added a Greek fisherman's cap, we hurried out of the building lobby, graced as it was with a kind of prison lighting.

As would happen always in Manhattan, heads turned

everywhere we went. Only just whispered, such lines as these formed the obligato of our walks through the city: "It's Tennessee Williams! Can it be Tennessee Williams? He looks pretty good. He looks o.k. What's he doing here?" This was the celebrity coinage of the day.

"Mr. Williams," cried one intrepid member of the crowd. "What are you doing now?"

"We're about to put a new play upon the boards. I guess there's been no press here in New York about it. It's called *Clothes for a Summer Hotel*. It had pretty good notices in Chicago. My producers may be tempting fate, but it opens on my birthday, which is this March 26th."

Fans were often astounded by the length of time and the depth of information he would provide for these· brief encounters. And, no matter how preoccupied he was, he never cold-shouldered an autograph seeker.

Arriving at the restaurant, Tennessee created a slight stir among the apathetic help. We were quickly guided to a good table.

"There are some advantages to being a celebrity, I suppose," said Tennessee. Indeed, his celebrity was rapidly heating up with the imminent Broadway opening of the play. His face, in photographs which no friend would have released to the media, glared balefully from the covers of many New York literary and arts papers. I came to have the habit of double-checking his living image as we walked the streets of Manhattan with the portraits which peered from the stands of virtually every news vendor in New York. I determined that someone had roused him suddenly from a hungover sleep and taken all these ghastly pictures at one time, and then, with true thoughtfulness, submitted them to every possible media outlet. I could think of no other explanation. Certainly, Tennessee did look much better in the flesh than in these pictures.

"You don't really look that 'morning after' all the time

Tennessee. Where did these people get those terrible photographs? Don't you have someone controlling this kind of thing?"

"I don't mean to saddle you with the unobtainable right off, baby. But that's one reason why I wanted you here. I feel that I'm at a considerable disadvantage on my own. We're going to check up on all these people who are allegedly in my employ. We're just going to check into the p.r. end of things, my agents, and my attorneys. I'm just too tired to do it all by myself. You're like an undemanding brother to me. I know you can help me. That is, if you still want to."

"Oh, Tennessee, I know you're going to make it as difficult as possible. But we'll get the job done, somehow."

We both laughed at this assay into reality.

At dinner, Tennessee gradually unveiled his plans. There were to be some surprises to come, to say the least of it, but he held to his own dramatic timetable for revelation and his hand was not to be tipped before the significant moment. For tonight, he had determined that we were just good friends, catching up at a restaurant, under no undue duress.

In the mood that seemed to set the tone of Manhattan, our waiter was high in attitude and low in performance. He did not seem to wish to partake in Tennessee's famous drinking habits, even to the point of providing a glass of wine.

"Stags Leap, baby," Tennessee said to the waiter.

"I beg your pardon? Did you want to order something or not?" said the waiter.

"I was under the impression that I just had, you know," said Tennessee.

"Stags Leap is a cabernet sauvignon," I said to the waiter. "Do you have it on your list?" I was pleased that

Tennessee was learning about good wines. Stags Leap was his Chicago wine.

"I don't have it and have never heard of it. If you want red wine then have the house red," offered our obliging waiter.

"It would seem to be the simpler way," said Tennessee. And bring my friend his J & B. He's a confirmed Scotch man."

The waiter was almost paralyzed as he realized Tennessee had implied that he could even begin to care what either of us really might want.

"New York waiters," I said laconically.

"They think we can see through their present occupation to the fancied day when their names are in lights on Broadway. I have no such powers, in any event," Tennessee lamented in his amusing manner.

Tennessee was looking well. It was amazing how journalistic photographers could never catch him on a good day. Too, he was bright and brisk in his behavior, though a certain melancholy underscored his ongoing good humor. He was dressing in a businesslike way in a conservative two-piece suit and a modest, tasteful tie.

Encouraged by his attire as much as his mood, I suggested we assign priorities to our New York, pre-opening activities. But here again Tennessee proved evasive. He seemed to eschew any kind of organization, even if it obviously meant simplifying some of the drearier aspects of life for him. All activities must be conducted allusively, as he had gone to some pains to communicate during our first Chicago period.

I advanced the notion of an organized approach to the press.

"I'm convinced that some favorable publicity could help the ticket sales, as it did in Chicago. But here in New York it may be all over but the weeping, baby. All over but the weeping."

Even if that were true, as we both supposed it might well be, we still had to live through the events to come in some manner approaching optimism. I was determined that we would do whatever we could no matter what the prevailing mood of New York journalism.

"We'll work on it, baby. Let's just relax and enjoy our dinner, if our waiter will ever oblige us by taking our order for it. We have reservations for lunch at Romeo del Salta tomorrow, at noon. We're meeting a friend of mine from London. It's important that you meet."

As the last person Tennessee had said it was important I meet was Geraldine Page, I assumed we were in for something approaching a psychodrama.

Rather wearily, I said, "And who am I to meet? Who is this friend from London?"

"The Lady Maria St. Just. She's probably my oldest living friend. We've had our ups and downs throughout the years, as you may have noted in my *Memoirs*. She insists on coming to my openings, no matter how sad the occasion may prove to be. To add interest to the occasion, she's bringing in her two daughters. I could hardly say no, under the circumstances. After all, they are my goddaughters."

"And what role have you assigned them in these proceedings, Tennessee?"

"We'll try to keep it simple. She has insisted on lunch tomorrow. She has heard of you. You may expect that she'll vet you. I told her you'd be up to it."

"It won't be as simple as it sounds, Tennessee, and you know it. Shouldn't we be spending time with your agents and trying to get something meaningful done instead?"

"Oh, you'll find Maria meaningful, baby. Don't worry about that. But we'll get to the agents, too."

Tennessee was still on his fighter's regimen.

"Red meat's the ticket, baby," he said, as he ordered a filet. Beef protein would assume mythical proportions on this Manhattan voyage. No one could argue that stamina was very much what was called for now.

As we wandered the Broadway streets after dinner, fans left us in a wake of whispers.

"I like having you here, baby," he said. "I feel safe enough to walk around this town. And that's no small compliment to you. Let's walk as much as time allows while you're here."

"Sure, Tennessee, we'll walk a lot while we're here."

We had a nightcap back at the apartment. Tennessee went to his desk and typed for a while. I went to my room to read. Beside the bed was a copy of his book of poems *Androgyne Mon Amour.* As I read the lyrical, haunting, and, yes, dirge-like lines, I heard their author still typing in the next room.

I fell asleep to its sound.

CHAPTER VIII

Days of Justice I

THERE WAS SCARCELY DAWN light available to see Tennessee as he shook me awake the next morning. It was obviously raining out, for his coyote parka was wet and smelled like a wet dog.

"What's happening, Tennessee? Where have you been?"

"Out shopping, baby."

"At this hour? What time is it, anyway?"

"Five or 5:30 thereabouts. I'm going to start writing now, but I wanted to get us some things." He had placed a brown paper bag on the end of the bed and held out a box towards me. "You'll need something to wear here other than those Milan suits you wear, baby. Open it up and try it on."

Tennessee knew I hated early mornings, but I had come to believe that in this, as in other aspects of the education he envisioned for me, I would have to alter my thinking. I opened the box. It contained a beautiful black leather jacket.

"Put it on, baby. Let's see if it fits right."

So I stood up in my shorts and put on the black leather jacket. It was a good fit.

"It's great, Tennessee. I've always wanted one but always wondered if it was really 'me.' "

"To all indications, it is. You may as well try to be comfortable while you're here. It won't be easy, but we'll make it as easy as we can." He grabbed the bag at the end of the bed. "You're a J & B man as I remember," he said, gesturing to me with a bottle of the Scotch. "I got myself some red wine, though I have serious doubts as to whether it's any you'd approve of," he said, peering at the label of one of the bottles he had bought.

"Isn't it a little early for all this? How did you find a black leather jacket and those bottles of booze at this hour?"

"It's that old Manhattan magic, baby. That old Manhattan magic," he chuckled. "But go back to bed and get some rest. I hope my typing doesn't bother you, but it's what I do every morning, no matter what. I'll wake you later in time for our lunch with the Lady St. Just. Maybe you'd better save that black leather jacket for another occasion, baby."

It was now about 6:00 A.M. I heard the sound of a reluctant cork popping and then the regular sound of typing. I learned to fall asleep to its sound.

Tennessee was in the shower when I next awoke. I walked about the apartment, made some coffee, and thought to make some notes for the day's activities. It was abundantly clear that some rein had to be put on the flow of things or the day might evaporate into a distillation of almost pure illusion.

As I searched for a clean piece of writing paper amid the tangle of materials on Tennessee's writing table, the puritanism in my Midwestern heart registered a kind of horror at the vision before me. Classic pieces of crumpled writer's paper retold in song and dance in so many writer's tales formed small hills among the other debris upon the table. Near to the typewriter were what I presumed were the pages of Tennessee's morning labors. They were all spattered with wine. Disorganization was a word gone pale in this light.

Tennessee emerged all bright and brisk, showered hair tousled and his fighter's terrycloth robe bound haphazardly about him. "Pretend you're looking at the ruins of a civilization," he said bemusedly. "I really need someone to try to organize that stuff. Maybe while you're here . . ."

"Coffee, Tennessee?"

"At this hour? It's late and we have a lunch date. Could you just help me with something here in the kitchen?"

A bottle of wine lay askew in the basin of the kitchen sink. A corkscrew emerged from the battered cork at a rakish angle. Tennessee indicated the scene of his skirmish with the bottle. "Is it hopeless, or can you redeem the situation?"

The incident was redeemed and we prepared for the lunch ahead.

"We will arrive early," said Tennessee. "We will seat the table with me between you and Maria. In that way I can try to referee."

"Referee?"

"Well, you see, Maria's a hard case. We're going to have to listen to her side of the story and then go ahead and do what we want anyway."

"Tennessee, do you really need me there? If it's a reunion, surely you should be alone together?"

"I do not wish to be alone with Maria. She cannot be ignored. After all, she's flown herself and her two daughters

here at considerable expense to herself. No, we must proceed and see what she has to say."

"All I know of Maria St. Just is what I remember reading
in your *Memoirs*. You keep saying that you'll talk about
your relationship with her at some further time in the
book, but you never did get around to it. From the book, I
know she must be a member of the British peerage and
resides in a townhouse in London and a large country house
on the Salisbury plain."

"The Salisbury plain? Is that the way it's identified?"

"It's been a crucial site throughout British history, not
just the Stonehenge incident, to which you refer in your
Memoirs."

"Well, it obviously continues to be a site crucial to
British history if the Lady St. Just has taken up residence
there. I just don't want another feud with her, you know.
They take so much out of me and they're never really
resolved."

"I'll go with you if you arm me with some more information about her," I said.

"Maria and I go back quite a while. She was Maria
Britneva, a White Russian peasant, or so I presume. She
has had ambitions as an actress through the years although
she has yet to make her mark in that capacity, you might
say [chuckle]."

"We could simplify this if you could just tell me if you
think she means you well or if she's bound to be another
burden during this opening."

"Let's just say she presents herself on pivotal occasions.
Since she's here with her daughters, I can't ignore her. She's
been of some friendship and help in the past and I think
you should just make up your mind to come on along to
this lunch."

"I'm here for you, Tennessee, so o.k. And the Lady St.
Just as an actress?"

"I hear tell that her career was terminated—or at least substantially interrupted—because of an incident involving Dame Edith Evans. They might have been in *The Importance of Being Ernest,* but I can't remember if that was precisely the vehicle. In any event, Dame Edith wore somewhat heroic dentures, which caused her to spit a bit when she proclaimed her lines. Finally, when she could bear no more, Maria took up a pillow during one of their scenes together and pushed it into Dame Edith's face, to stifle the flow. The British don't take kindly to having their Dames of the British Empire smothered upon the stage and Maria was at some unsuccessful pains to explain her—of course—spontaneous behavior. I don't believe she's acted since."

"Any more insights into her winning ways, Tennessee?"

"She did behave very badly in the affair of the long dissolution of my relationship with my agent, Audrey Wood. Of course, Maria doesn't have the faintest notion I know anything about this particular episode."

"I seem to remember from your *Memoirs* that you finally split with Audrey Wood during the Chicago production of *Out Cry* in the early seventies."

"That's true. But Maria had been working away at Audrey for at least a decade before that. During some of my blackest days back in the sixties Maria took it upon herself to spread the word in London that I was dropping Miss Wood as my agent. This caused considerable heartache for Audrey and certainly didn't make my days any easier."

"Why would Maria want you to sever your ties to Audrey Wood?"

"Perhaps to stand alone in my affections, do you think? Cousin Jim calls her the Spider Woman, perhaps with some reason. As I think about it, she seems to have appeared only at my blackest moments and with the greatest determination to assert herself. That would seem to fit the pattern, wouldn't it, baby? She never really does anything significant to help in any real way. But she is there. Perhaps she hopes to find me in such a weakened condition one day that I'll surrender my power of attorney to her, as well. We have to think about that."

"But aren't we planning to see your attorneys within the next few days?"

"Yes, the Eastmans are awaiting our call. I've asked for an update on the state of my fortunes, financial and otherwise."

"Well, perhaps we should mention your concerns regarding the Lady St. Just."

"It's all speculation at this juncture. She has worked her way into my will, though. To a pretty tune, at that. Royalties from two plays will go to her. She and Rose will get most everything."

"From what you've told me, this is all most ominous. She must consider this Broadway opening a black moment. Shall we expect the worst?"

"You have a black sense of humor, somewhat akin to my own, baby."

"Well, you couldn't keep me from meeting her, now, Tennessee. And what have you told her about me?"

"About you, baby? Just a little bit. Enough to pique her interest, perhaps to arouse a little edge of fear. When she heard I had a new male friend, she of course assumed that you were another boyfriend, with no credentials, to be blown off at her whim. She does work against all my relationships with men, I am aware of that. But I deflated her expectations just a bit by telling her that you were in business and had had a successful publishing background. She says she's most interested to meet you, but I can tell she holds out little hope for me in any regard. Oh, one more consideration, baby. The one thing she does try to do that can only meet with universal approbation is to try to stop my drinking. We'll stop for our pre-luncheon cocktails elsewhere before we present ourselves at lunch. There, you will witness me nurse a single glass of wine throughout the ordeal."

As we walked through Manhattan for our "ordeal," Tennessee had an unusually brisk and determined air about him. We stopped, as he had said we would, for pre-luncheon cocktails in a dark little lounge in the Hotel Winslow.

As we settled at the bar, Tennessee said, "Judy Garland used to drink here. She thought no one could see her. Ha, ha! Perhaps we will be more fortunate."

Just as the reading in Chicago at the Newberry had required the judicious consumption of double martinis, the ordeal ahead of us did the same. Braced with his two doubles, we moved ahead to our meeting with destiny at Romeo Salta.

We had just been seated at our booth, when Maria St. Just arrived. "Ten, darling," she gushed. "Of course, you're that business person Ten has brought along. Good. Very good. Now, Ten, what is going on here? Is the play going o.k.? You said it did well in Chicago. Fine. But is everything being done that can be done here in New York?" She looked towards me, expectantly. Tennessee looked into the tablecloth.

Maria St. Just had an unfortunate hatchet face which, while it asserted quite aggressively that it would brook no affront to its dignity, at the same time it betrayed her inmost culpabilities. I'm afraid that the knowing concern of a friend one might have hoped to see traced in her features was hard lined out into blatant self-concern.

"I only just arrived last night, Maria. Tennessee has been filling me in on what to expect here. I have asked how I can help, if in any way I can. Perhaps you could help us, too. You've been through these openings before and must be familiar with what goes on. Will you help us by telling me what you can about these affairs?"

"Well, I'll do what I can. Ten, Franco (to me: 'Zefferelli') just called me at Voglis' and wishes you the very best. He's doing a film in Italy. I explained I had to be here with you. He understood."

"Do you mean Franco required your presence on the set in Italy?" inquired Tennessee, giving me one of his sly, bemused looks, which Maria did not miss.

"I am in touch with Franco on all that is important to him, you know that. Now, what are we going to do here, before the opening? Let's look at the menus, shall we, Ten?"

"You will be pleased to know that we have not been aimlessly shuffling about, awaiting your arrival, Maria. Bruce and I have been catching up and have begun to schedule our activities. He seems to think we can actually make some headway against this reincarnation of the Manhattan project. I don't know, but I do like his hopefulness. There's spirit there, Maria, spirit."

"No doubt. Something simple for lunch, I think. How about you, Ten? Are you watching your weight? You look well enough. Still on your first glass of wine? Waiter! Waiter! Just the insalata verde for me. You might bring a Perrier."

We ordered promptly, so as not to miss a word of Maria's sparkling telegraphic commentary.

"Now, Tennessee, you could take some lessons in suits from your young friend here," she said. She gave my attire an appraising glance. "Can't you try to put yourself out a little more and get some clothes suitable to your condition?"

Tennessee glanced at me, appeared to be evaluating my wardrobe. "This is a new suit, Maria. I just bought it in Chicago when I was there for *Clothes*. Is it really that bad?"

"You look like a travelling salesman, Ten. Bruce, take him shopping this afternoon and pick out something distinguished for him. This is your sixty-ninth birthday and the opening, too. You really can't look like this."

Tennessee looked fine. Perhaps not fashionably attired, but I thought he looked quite well, rather in the manner of a college professor who does have other things to think about.

"Well, Maria," I said, "be grateful for the suit. During the Chicago run we had a Yves St. Laurent jogging suit. That was his signature attire for that trip. I have just assumed that Tennessee was more or less beyond these things."

"If you don't want to do it, I will try to find the time. I have my daughters to dress for the opening, as well as myself. But I really think a fine new suit would be just the right thing for the occasion."

"Maria," said Tennessee, "we are trying here to open my play, you know. I brought Bruce here to help me with that and to give me some support. I'm glad you like the way he dresses. I do, too, but we have other considerations just now."

"Have you been to see Milton?" asked Maria.

Tennessee groaned. "We haven't done anything except get the lay of the land as best we could. Do you think we should bother with Milton?"

Turning to me, Maria said, "Do you know Milton? Milton Goldman? ICM. Larry Olivier's agent. The best. You must go see him, you simply must go see him."

"If Tennessee wishes to see Milton Goldman, then we should," I said.

"Let's not play games," said Tennessee. "That little visit will do very little good. So far as I know, they impede my progress rather than advance it."

"What nonsense, Tennessee," said Maria. "They always have your best interests at heart. Audrey is never allowed in the way, since they know how you feel about her. There's no reason why you should think Mitch Douglas isn't doing a good job for you."

"The last time I tried to have a meeting with Mitch Douglas," said Tennessee, "it was allowed as how he was unavailable for me because he was attending a college reunion. A college reunion in which he had a starring role, it would seem, as he's the visiting hero telling all about all the famous people he represents."

"Bruce," said Maria severely, "if you succeed in nothing else you must get Ten to Milton. He's just in one of his moods. I knew I had to be here. I'll go right now to phone Milton and make an appointment for right after lunch. See that Ten is there. No, we'll all go."

Maria left the table. Tennessee turned to me with a bemused chuckle. "You'll love this experience, baby. It's like going to see the Pope."

Our arrival at International Creative Management was met with a great scurrying of receptionists and clerks. Having decided to indulge Maria with this visit, Tennessee was not about to observe the formalities of sitting in the waiting room for Milton Goldman. He grabbed me by the arm and we marched towards Goldman's office, Maria hurrying behind.

A diminutive figure with gray hair pulled back in a bun looked in our direction, assumed a terrified expression on her face, and hurried out of our sight.

"Ha, Tennessee, there she is. Did you see her? It was Audrey Wood. Too frightened to stay and greet you."

At this juncture we were entering Milton Goldman's office. We were just in time to see Goldman removing a set of books from the shelves to the right of his desk and replacing them with another set of matched volumes, rather in the manner of a collected works. When he realized we were in the room, he paled for a moment but soon rallied with just the kind of corporate enthusiasm that I knew Tennessee hated above all other false human conventions.

"We just saw Audrey Wood, but only briefly," said Tennessee.

"Now, Tennessee," said Milton Goldman. "Let's just say how happy we are that you're here. When I heard you were coming, I put a call into Moe [Maureen Stapleton]. She'll be calling any minute now to tell you how happy we all are that you're back in New York."

"I'm here for a reason, you know," said Tennessee. "I have a play to open and if past experience is any guide— and it always is in my sad experience—it's going to be rough sailing. Can you tell us anything of what's been done to promote this play of mine? This is Bruce Smith. I brought him here because he knows about publicity and I hoped he could help sort things out. As you know, we had a fairly successful run in Chicago."

"Tennessee, I have no need to tell you again that you are my favorite author among those we represent. Just look up there (he indicated the newly-placed bound set). I always keep your collected works by me as I work. So, of course, you have all our attention. What can we do for you?"

"Perhaps Bruce could answer that question more intelligently than I," said Tennessee.

Goldman turned his attention to me, his hands together in a thoughtful, clerical manner.

"It would be helpful if we could have a printout showing what advertising is planned and what kind of pre-opening

publicity we can anticipate. Tennessee has checked into the
box office and sales are quite slow. Does the general public
even know *Clothes* is opening in a few days?"

"Well, I'm sure there's an advertising program of some
kind. And there must be some kind of publicity planned.
I'll ask Mitch to see whom you can talk to about it."

The phone rang. "It's Moe!" cried Milton Goldman.
"Maureen, darling, your favorite author is sitting right
here. Would you like to speak with him?"

"Just ask her to call me at the apartment, if you would be
so kind," said Tennessee.

Somewhat crestfallen that this little offering had failed
to please, Goldman said, "Maureen, darling, you just call
him later at his apartment, will you? You'll be at the
opening? At the party? Fine. Goodbye."

Tennessee led us in rising hastily from our seats. "You
know I want some information, Milton. I'm asking you to
give it to Bruce. Have someone call him at the apartment
by tomorrow morning." Without further ceremony we left
ICM. On the way to Eastman and Eastman, Tennessee's
legal representatives, we saw Truman Capote advancing
towards us.

"Truman," screamed Maria. "Truman."

We approached the meeting point. Truman Capote
looked vaguely at Tennessee and me and gave a weak smile.
He briefly turned his head to Maria and looked at her as
though he had never seen her before. He passed on by.

"Has Truman lost all his teeth, do you suppose?" asked
Tennessee. "From that weak smile I would say he may have
lost them all." We walked on a bit.

"Now, Maria, you must have a million things to do. We
simply cannot detain you any further. We're on our way to
Eastman's. We'll talk later. Perhaps dinner?"

Maria grimaced and left us.

"I told you when we first met in Key West that they'd all prefer me dead," said Tennessee. "All this play-acting. We're no further ahead of the game than we were before we wasted time with these people. Perhaps I did learn something about Audrey, though. Running away like that. Remind me to look something up in my files at the apartment. There might be something there."

"O.K. Do we have an appointment with Eastman and Eastman, or are we just going to stop by unannounced?"

"A little surprise might be in order, I think. I recently switched to them on a dear friend's advice. I'd like to get a clearer picture of what they do."

We were received by the Eastmans, both Lee and John. I felt some relief almost immediately. These people looked civilized, sensible, intelligent, and actually spoke in whole sentences. It was like a breath of spring, with all its hopefulness, to meet them. It was my impression that they were truly concerned about Tennessee.

But by that time Tennessee was worn to an electric frazzle by the day's events. He had no more patience for polite conversation. He literally pushed Lee Eastman from behind his desk and shouted into the room one name. "Voglis!" he cried as though the waters were rising about him. "VOGLIS!"

John Eastman, the son, retrieved a telephone number for the otherwise unidentified Voglis, but Tennessee proved unable to dial it. The receptionist tried the number. There was no answer. Tennessee was now in a rage of frustration. "Get me out of here. Get me out of here. I just can't stand this any more."

The Eastmans consoled me with sympathetic expressions as I hurried with Tennessee through the door.

I had learned that day just what Tennessee could take and just how much of it.

CHAPTER IX

Days of Justice II

THE PROFOUND INTERMESHING OF Tennessee's life and art as expressed in *Clothes for a Summer Hotel* was undeniable. He called the play his "ghost play." And just as, in the play, Scott Fitzgerald is frustrated in his appeal to gain entrance to the asylum which holds Zelda, Tennessee was kept from having any real control over the events which were to have such a traumatic impact on what was left of his life. In most depictions, ghosts seem to be attired in light and billowing garb. Tennessee's words for these were the title of his last big play. Now, he was garbed with a too-thin emotional raiment for the onslaught of the New York theatre world. In some very real ways, he would catch his death of it.

When we returned to his apartment that afternoon, Tennessee ambled about restlessly. He said, "You see, it is as I said it was in Key West. They have tried to deal with me by treating me as a ghost, which of course implies that I am already dead, which is what they clearly wish me to be. Because being ghostly isn't sufficient unto the day, baby. I have asked you here to help me out. As a friend, I know there is only so much you can do with this seemingly irretrievable situation. But (and here he looked up at me with that now familiar worn, torn smile of his), let's do what we can. There may be some surprises in store for them yet."

"Clothes for a summer hotel may be what ghosts wear to dinner, baby, but you will oblige me deeply if you'll remove that Armani suit just for this evening and get into some jeans and that black leather jacket I got for you. A change of attire can often signal a break in a spell. We must do what we can since we're to meet the Lady St. Just for dinner. A black leather jacket may be just the theatrical bit of business we need to set her straight."

Tennessee laughed his deep laugh of appreciation and wicked delight when I presented myself for the evening's rehearsal and dinner in levis and leather jacket. "If nothing else," he said, "it should cut short the evening with Maria."

We arrived at the Cort Theatre no further ahead of the game than we had been earlier in the day. Tennessee's wish for a new Scott went unregarded. And Tennessee had decided there was no real hope for Geraldine Page to match Zelda as he had envisioned her, so he had, the day before, written in a reference to insulin intake at the asylum by way of explanation for her bloated appearance. At least that suggestion stuck and the new lines were entered into the script.

"I feel as though I'm just going through the paces, you know," said Tennessee. "The producer, Elliott Martin, and his wife are in town. Perhaps we can talk to them about adequately representing this play to its public."

"Let's do that after we've reviewed the leads given us today," I said.

"If Milton Goldman and ICM have anything to do with it, you can be quite calm. Nothing whatever will happen. Their achievement is by pure osmosis."

The rehearsal went well. Its pace seemed to have been tightened. New language had been introduced, which Tennessee duly noted. "At least they're implementing my notes, so all control has not passed from me," he said.

At the curtain, we went backstage for a little chat with the stars, particularly Ms. Page. More sullen than ever, she greeted us with a grimace at her dressing room door. Attempting to introduce an element of common humanity to the proceedings, Tennessee inquired after his two godsons, Geraldine's children. "You won't be seeing them this trip, Tennessee," was all she said, cryptically.

The disheveled and even more morose José Quintero stood damp and wrapped in a black leather trench coat at the door to the lobby. "Good evening, José," said Tennessee. "A good evening for a gallows hanging."

Quintero grunted and bowed his head, turning away into the night. "José seems a mess, Tennessee," I said.

"A mess? Well, he's obviously returned to the bottle for solace on this sad occasion. But let's remember he's a human being, baby, a human being."

"Why won't you be seeing your godsons, Tennessee? Are they away?" I inquired.

"Oh, no, baby. Ms. Geraldine Page has taken it into her head that, given my acknowledged perversions and addictions, I am not suitable company for my godsons. She refuses me admittance to them. Do you think she thinks I have some dark sexual interest in them? I never cared for children, particularly in that way. I think we can just say that Ms. Page has her priorities and let's just leave it at that."

I knew Tennessee was deeply hurt by this continued emotional onslaught from Geraldine Page. But now, as we entered what he called "the final stages" of production, such details simply became mired in the overall depression he was experiencing.

"Only Maria would feel that this was some kind of festive occasion which called for an evening at Elaine's," said Tennessee. "But, I said we'd meet her there. I wish we could just go to some dark spot with some pleasant music, a nice filet, some wine, and hide," he said in his somewhat defeated, morosely humorous vein.

Instead, we made our visitation to Elaine's, where Maria had secured a "celebrity table" on the strength of Tennessee's name. Seated next to us was Woody Allen and his party. Allen was clearly aware of Tennessee's identity, but Tennessee did not recognize him. In a loud voice, Maria observed, "There's Woody Allen, Ten." "What? Who?" he said. "Oh surely you know Woody Allen, Ten," Maria went on. In that Allen's table was not four feet away, he of course, heard all this, but made no attempt to break into the private world of Tennessee's table. The gulf was recognized as insurmountable and left at that.

Fatigued as we all were by the mounting tensions of the Broadway opening, this quick foray into the world of show biz Manhattan lasted just as long as it took to consume some indifferent pasta and a single bottle of wine. Maria wished to go on to Joe Allen's or some such, but the evening's proceedings were brought to a definitive halt by Tennessee.

"As surely you can understand, Maria, I am exhausted and must have my faculties about me for the work we have ahead of us tomorrow. To my knowledge, nothing's been done by my highly paid associates to promote this play of mine, which will, in all probability, be my swan song to the theatre. Good night, Maria."

Simply to break the steely skein of grim inevitability

which seemed to be governing our day, we decided to have a nightcap in a little boite on the East Side before returning to the confinement of the apartment. "These simple gestures are so disapproved of by everyone around us," said Tennessee. "Which wouldn't bother me so much if it weren't all so hypocritical. How do you think Gerry attained her present appearance? Not by a diet of prawns and yogurt."

Indeed, stopping in at a pub on the way home did lift the spirits. Just to be among people who were alien to the present chore was a relief in itself. Away from it all, Tennessee brightened considerably and became quite voluble. "I've always hated New York," he said. "And now it seems my way of repaying the compliment. It was bearable when Frankie was alive, but as he declined so did my love affair with Manhattan, as ambivalent as that was. You have to be young and in astounding good health to put up with this place. Unfortunately, I seem to be singularly unable to bring these requirements to the party."

As it had from the beginning of this Manhattan rendezvous, it rained constantly in a desultory fashion. Nonetheless, we walked on through it to the apartment. When we reached home, Tennessee scrambled for his identification card, without which one could not pass through the turnstiles which were presided over by armed guards. "I seem to have left my pass to this establishment in my rooms," said Tennessee. "Can you let us in?" "Only with proper identification," said the guard.

Life often presents occasions when repressed rage and frustration can be turned to good advantage. "If you don't know who this tenant is," I said, "then you're the only person in Manhattan who doesn't. Now stop this stupidity and let us in."

It worked. It was one of our few victories in Manhattan,

but we good humoredly treasured it as we rose with the
usual sycophants in the elevator to our floor.

Frank Merlo's photographic portrait was the first you
would see as you entered the apartment, and its placement
there was surely no accident. Frankie still welcomed Tennessee home, with his warm, handsome, and easy smile.

We kept the lights down and sipped some wine. The
lights of Manhattan stirred up through the mist and the
traffic sounds, blissful symbol of some rest at last. "Let me
wander back a bit," said Tennessee. "Let me sort of sum up
what I feel about this opening and its effect on me. It's no
different than other openings I've had here. The real differ-
ence is that now I know I'm coming to my own end of
things. I know you don't interpret this, as many do, as the
sentimental cadgings of an old man. In some way I do
know this is the end, or nearly the end, of my time here."

We were quiet for a few minutes and then he began to
speak again.

"You are helpful to me because there is so much understanding without the need of so much speech," Tennessee
said. "I know you understand much of what I'm feeling
without the need for me to express it verbally, which takes a
great weight from me, a responsibility that I need not feel.
I know I'm in the final stages now and I need all my
energies for my plays. Promise me we'll have the courage to
follow through on a plan I made long ago and somehow
have never had the nerve to follow through."

"You have a plan, Tennessee? Something that will help
you now, with *Clothes?*"

"With the play and with me, emotionally. You've seen
what a jungle the theatre world is. Everyone on their worst
behavior. Most of them behave unspeakably to me, but
we've discussed that issue before. But since the whole
issue, the whole play really begins with me, I feel responsi-

ble. I feel that I try to rise above the pettiness and rancor, if only to help the play."

"Wouldn't it take the patience of a saint to behave in a cool, collected manner with all this mendacity—your word—rampant about us?"

"It's almost inevitable to become misanthropic in this business. I've tried, I think, valiantly, to overcome it because I think it limits my ability to work correctly. A psychiatrist with whom I worked some years ago asked me, 'When will you know an honest man when you meet one?' I don't mean to be sentimental, but I think I've met one now. In some way you touch my soul and, more agnostically perhaps, I realize that there is no reason for you to be with me except for genuine concern. You're not in the theatre; you have your own life; you must be here because you want to be. Your work for me in Chicago was a fantastic gesture of sympathy and friendship. It will always be appreciated for it hints at and lets me remember the honesty and good faith and true affection of all my friends and collaborators. It helps me believe, as I know I can, in some good things in people."

Though our relationship did exist largely on the basis of a silent, intuitive understanding, it was a great relief to hear that understanding affirmed so clearly.

"Since we're verbalizing, Tennessee, can you lay out your wishes for this specific New York time for me? There's so much confusion out there that, forgive the expression, a 'game plan' would be helpful. What are your plans, contingency and otherwise?"

"You are right to help me assert myself more strongly about the play, Bruce. Though they wish me out of the play, certain commitments I have made for myself are preeminent. But you could help me accept, as courteously as possible, whether I solicit it or not, advice, no matter who offers it. But at the same time we must remember that I have the longest acquaintance with the play and I must not place anyone else's counsel regarding the script above my own counsel."

"I've always considered that an unnegotiable position, Tennessee. It really shouldn't be open to question."

"But at times I retreat because it sometimes seems that everyone else seems to be working but me. When I am just attending rehearsals, I must remind myself that for two or three years I was the solitary worker: all those working mornings—the bad ones when I wondered if a good working day would ever come again. With all these pressures upon me, I must try to remember that bittersweet time when my life was the play and the play was my life. When I bring this remembrance to bear, I don't have to feel ashamed of my passivity during rehearsal time. I mustn't let them all make me feel that I'm an outsider to my own play."

"I think I've understood that, Tennessee. Though I would never presume to speak for you, I do, when the occasion arises, state simply that, after all you are the writer, the author. Sometimes these simple facts have to be asserted with all these wild theatrical egos flying about."

"I try to be neither too humble nor too arrogant, too unbending nor too pliant. But should I be compelled to choose a position in this matter, you can help me get up on my 'high horse.' "

"With the greatest pleasure, always, Tennessee."

"But remind me, if I forget it, that I am working with creative artists whose dedication, presumably, to this play and its production, is at least equal to my own, from their own personal perspective. It's helpful if I try to be grateful to them, to be considerate of the pride they take in their work."

"Tennessee, it's difficult to remember that these are serious people when they act like spoiled, irresponsible children. They wouldn't last a day in any normal profession."

"Take into account their innate insecurity, baby. No matter how assured they may seem, they need, as much as I, as much reassurance one fighting man can give to the other in the foxhole we call the stage."

"What do you really think we can anticipate from the New York drama critics?"

"Whatever we get in that regard, I have to remember that I am a highly personal playwright and offer arenas of human experience and auras of feeling which must seem very foreign and even offensive to many in the audience, including those critics you mention. Let's try to retain our equilibrium if once again I'm called morbid or that my play is just another 'fetid swamp.' What I offer in my plays is a translation of my own, personal world into the terms of the larger world. The differences then appear for what they are: simply varied shadows of the same subject. Because it is my choice, or even my destiny to do this, I really must expect no special clemency or dispensation, as it were. I certainly don't wish or deserve the special attention paid to the halt or the blind.

"My own personal aging and the state of my health plays no small role in this troublesome production here. But I still have it in me to present myself as a 'tough old bird.' Plump character actors with unruly mustaches have never been successful in the roles of either Joan of Arc or Camille. I must realize my limitations."

"Since we're having this conversation, Tennessee, what do you wish to do if the critics don't support the play?"

"You're here to help me have the courage to flee this city, even before the reviews are out. I want to give everything I can to the production and then beat it, baby. Don't forget that. My travel agent's number is on the desk. Just book us out when I say so."

"Won't Maria interfere with these plans? She's already planned a cast party and there's another at some restaurant for your birthday."

"The Lady St. Just can do the honors for me, then. I must avoid it all. I want to be at work on my next play before I even see the notices. That's what I've been working on here. *Masks Outrageous and Obscure.* I have to be caught up in it to sustain me through the reviews."

"But Maria already has a contingency planned, which she whispered to me at ICM. You're to go on TV to attempt to counteract the reviews."

"Remember me on TV? Twitching my eyebrows and licking my dry lips and speaking with what the straight world indulgently calls my 'slight lisp.' They think it's a sexual giveaway, but actually I acquired it when my real teeth were replaced by a bridge made by a chain store dentist during a period of enforced economic retrenchment in California. Keep me away from it all! Let's be booked already! Via jet plane, away to somewhere, away, away!"

"I'll try to keep you to your word, Tennessee."

"An interesting turn of phrase. We must do it. We must."

I hoped the new jacket, this neat symbol, slung across the chair would be enough for us both, for life and play continued as one. Spring had arrived, but Tennessee had only packed for the summer.

CHAPTER X

Days of Justice Part III

"ARE YOU AMBULATORY?" CAME Tennessee's call from the next room. It was barely dawn. But Tennessee was struggling with a paper wrapper and, I gathered, losing the round. "I need help with this package."

I opened the package for Tennessee. Under the wrapping was an innocuous looking gray cardboard box. Before he moved to open that part of his present, he said, "You can go back to bed, baby. Conserve your strength. It's bound to be an eventful day, you know."

I took advantage of the reprieve. A few hours later I was showering, when the bathroom door opened. Tennessee said, "Don't think I wish to disturb you in your ablutions, but have you seen the alcohol, the isopropyl alcohol?"

"Have you wounded yourself, Tennessee? No, I haven't seen the isopropyl alcohol."

A quick rustling through the cabinets evidently produced the sought-after item. Then there was a sound of wrappers being opened and a more discreet sound of glass vials clinking against one another. There was silence. Then a turning on of the tap. After a moment, he said, "That rather prolonged shower you're taking will probably have to do for the day. We have a lot to do."

Tennessee left the room. I pulled back the shower curtain and there saw a still life I had hoped never to see in association with Tennessee. The sink and its edge were littered with hypodermic needles and unlabeled vials of fluids. Panic had set in for him. Red wine and the occasional martini had modulated into what appeared to be hard drugs. I wanted no part of it.

I rushed to dress. I found Tennessee typing.

"I want to write as much on my new play today as I possibly can. If the gods can be propitiated in any way, we must leave no stone unturned. You see, I'm living up to my promise to myself of last night. I'm going to be deep into my next work before the notices come out tonight." He was like a guilty child before a parent. He offered up his work in an attempt to shunt aside the drug issue.

I said, "Tennessee, you've left some things in the bathroom. If you're expecting any callers today, I'd suggest you tidy up a bit."

Studied silence. More typing. Looking up from his typewriter and turning to me, he said, "The great puritan asserts himself at last. Opening nights are always the acid test for true colors. Jim warned me you had this side to you. Don't you realize I have a play opening tonight?"

"Tennessee, I'm moving to a hotel for the duration. I think it would be a good idea. You might well wish to be alone to write and to conserve your energy."

"You move fast, baby. Well, that might be what the events call for. We'll both move into a hotel. I like the convenience of a hotel for my openings. I'll book us into the Alrae. Shall I specify separate floors?"

As usual, much communication went unspoken. I was relieved at the prospect of the privacy of a hotel, but I was unhappy at the evident rage of Tennessee's reaction to my response to the needle incident.

"I really don't want the details. I hope that stuff doesn't paralyze your ability to function through the opening."

"Shall we be civilized and turn to the events at hand?" he countered.

"We're obviously just candles in the wind, but I think we should make an attempt to see what kind of promotional effort has been put behind this play. Or, if your suspicions about your agents are correct, have they just determined to let *Clothes* sink or swim upon the merits of the reviews? I thought I'd run over to the Cort and check on the box office."

Tennessee sat bemused and unrepentant. He had determined that the forces of Broadway had set the noose. They were conspiring, as we moved onto the morning coffee, to sink the play and, if possible, kill off the playwright in the process.

He reached into his pocket and proffered a piece of crumpled paper. This he offered me in an offhand fashion.

"Here are some numbers you can call if your seeming taste for the bleak facts of life can be satisfied by the information you're so intent on acquiring."

I called the p.r. person identified on the list. In our brief conversation, she revealed herself to be a bold as brass, thoroughly nasty functionary, who, though a mere cipher in the corrupt stew of Broadway play production, still held a stranglehold on promotional programs for the play. She was adamant. No information was to be given to me, an outsider. Nor would she divulge anything to the play-

wright himself. This clone of Chicago's own media concierge came as no surprise. "If you think we're going to let
Mr. Williams have any say in this, you're totally naive,"
she said. Then she slammed down the phone.

After I passed on this rewarding exchange, Tennessee
said, "I know your puritan heart conceives of a special hell
for people like that, but unfortunately they are the rule,
not the exception. Frankie had the same result from them.
Just forget it. Now you know that Chicago doesn't have an
exclusive franchise on that kind of p.r. activity."

Despite his noble disclaimer, we both stood there
stunned for a moment, looking out the window into the
Manhattan mist. Of course, the rain continued to come
down.

I found it difficult to put this case down. We had
perused the New York dailies since we arrived and nothing
except small advertisements had appeared announcing the
play. Considering that this was Tennessee's first full-length
play since *Night of the Iguana* in the early 60's and that it
was backed by a preeminent, quality producer, it would
seem that some sort of media fanfare was called for. It had
been called for and issued in Chicago. I wondered now
more than ever why the play had ever been produced in the
first place. Not because of the quality of the play, but
because of the ambient anathema in which it and its author
seemed to be held.

"I told you that first night we met in Key West that
there was a pervasive attitude towards me in New York,
controlled, as best I can determine, by the *New York Times.*
They just don't want me around anymore. It's the age of
Neil Simon. That's a theatrical epitaph, baby, not an en-
dorsement." He could still chuckle.

"All we have going for the play is that oversize sandwich
board in front of the Cort Theatre with excerpts from

Claudia's favorable review. Thank God for that much. Certainly there's something else we could do."

"In my heyday, the sacrosanct *New York Times* used to print a big piece I'd write about the play's production; insights into the play, comments on the performers."

"If the *New York Times* is your avowed enemy, they'd hardly be likely to offer you any space to offer your interpretation of events."

In a neat turnabout, he said, "We can't rule them out. Give me an hour here at the typewriter. I'll have something for them we can drop off later."

I walked over to the Cort Theatre. Box office sales were disappointing. Advance ticket sales were almost exactly one half of what they had been in Chicago. It was my policy that, if we were to come through this extraordinary theatrical experience in one piece, Tennessee should be dealt nothing but truth, no matter how painful that truth might be. It was perhaps a mistake to dismiss the Blanche du Bois aspect of his personality, but I had no skill at shading lamplight with chiffon scarves in the manner of that heroine. I told Tennessee the bad news.

"My agents have let me down," he said. "Nothing tangible has been done in a positive way, but they'll all find a way to blame me. But, speaking of ICM, I've been pondering the strange behavior of Audrey Wood at their office yesterday. She rather deliberately tried to hide from me."

"As I remember you did fire her, Tennessee. She probably didn't want to be embarrassed," I said.

"She had to be fired, let go. Maria convinced me that she hadn't my true interests at heart. And now I'm convinced that she's guilty of something more than the betrayal of our friendship. Do you know Ray Stark?"

"He's a Hollywood producer. You think that Ray Stark and Audrey Wood conspired against you in some way?" I thought that perhaps the morning's injection had spurred on his innate paranoia.

"It was a most mysterious contract that she worked out with Ray Stark, who produced *Iguana*. She wrote up the whole document herself, without consulting me, thinking I was incompetent at the time, no doubt. By the terms of that contract, Stark could have made a cartoon out of *Iguana*. I was left with no artistic control at all."

"Is this your idea, Tennessee? Or is it fresh input from Maria St. Just?"

"We did discuss it on the phone this morning. We're going to have to get to the bottom of the situation now. I can't live with this implication hanging over my head."

"Your severance from Ms. Wood seems all of a tangle, but what happened to you and Billie Barnes? Even Maria allowed yesterday that she thought he had really tried to help you during some very difficult times. Wasn't he with you during the period you wrote your *Memoirs?*"

"I was always confused about Billie Barnes. He made me edgy. He did the strangest thing to me on the night of our first meeting, you know."

"What was that?"

"He told me that just the night before his lover had jumped from their balcony to his death. I'm terrified of physical violence of any kind. He must have known that. Why do you suppose he chose the occasion of our first meeting to tell me that terrible story?"

"Perhaps he just wanted to show you that he could get things done, Tennessee."

"Get things done!" His laughter was uproarious. The first I had heard since our relatively good days together in Chicago.

"Let's see what we can get done about the Wood/Stark conspiracy," he said, darkly.

"That episode, if it happened as you suggest, is more than fifteen years old, Tennessee. I don't think you could do anything about it even if you wanted to. Why don't you wait and talk to the Eastmans about it?"

"It's a moral issue now, not a judicial one at this point in time. If you're going to chronicle this cryptic chapter in my life you should have some perspective. You should know just how black the picture is, baby. You have to have perspective."

Resignedly, I said, "Where do we begin?"

"Over there," he shrugged rather indifferently to his desk. "I have a safe full of documents. It's evidence I want. It's not too late to do something about her. I'll expose this matter yet."

He was obviously beside himself with anxiety about the opening and seemed to be diverting his worry to something more safely in the past. But he was in a true fury.

"Call the building management, baby. We're going to burn the barn down if we have to over this matter."

The building manager arrived, in a great state of solicitude.

"I had a safe in this apartment," said Tennessee. "I had a safe and it is not here to all appearances. Now, do I call the authorities or do you deliver the safe?"

"If it's not here, it may be in your storage locker, Mr. Williams. I'll get my men on it right away," said the manager, cool under the circumstances.

Within one half hour, during which time Tennessee rifled through every drawer and cabinet in the apartment, the safe arrived. Of course, Tennessee did not have the combination, so the lock had to be forced, after he signed a document that said he was responsible and aware that this had occurred. His reputation had preceded him.

Files were hastily removed from the safe. "Look through

these," said Tennessee. "Look for anything signed by Ray Stark or Audrey Wood. These are the *Iguana* papers all right. What I want should be here."

I had no wish other than to see Tennessee safely through the opening of his play that night and then safely aboard a flight to Key West, if things went as we both silently expected and the play was savaged by the New York critics. So, I pretended to research the documents, but that was all. I had no wish to become involved in a dispute between Tennessee, Ray Stark, and Audrey Wood.

He soon tired of the search.

"We have to get that over to the *New York Times*," he said indicating his piece about *Clothes*. He had written it in my absence.

"We can leave it off on the way to lunch. We're due at your attorneys at 3:00 P.M. Perhaps we could plan to move to the hotel after that meeting."

"Trying to keep us to the safe and narrow, baby? Well, maybe that's called for." The apartment looked like it had experienced a visitation from a SWAT team, drawers pulled out, papers and documents strewn furiously around the room. It was, indeed, time to move on.

Tennessee had dressed for business in a conservative brown suit and simple tie. Under the circumstances, he looked rather calm, cool, and collected.

It was raining, and it would rain all day and all night. "Perfect day for the box office," Tennessee chuckled. "Can't you just see them lined up around the block vying for good seats to my play in this downpour?"

Strangely, we had a calm, discursive, and pleasant lunch. Tennessee confined himself to a single glass of red wine—always a good sign—and, when the check for our soup and sandwiches and a glass of wine each arrived in the amount of fifty-five dollars, Tennessee chuckled, pulling out his American Express card, which he regarded as his passport through the insanity that was his America.

"If you couldn't buy a suit for this amount just a few years ago, you could at least begin looking. Forgive me, but money, just cold hard cash, is on my mind just now. I want to see what the Eastman family says I'm worth. We'll find that out this afternoon. I plan to spring that request on them."

"Don't you trust the Eastmans, either, Tennessee?" I asked.

"Until proven or perhaps even just suspected of being guilty. They come highly recommended. The daughter is married to that Beatle Paul McCartney and they represent several other artists other than myself, Wilhelm de Koonig among them."

The waiter returned with the American Express slip to sign and returned his card. Holding it up, he laughed. "It's just my perverse sense of humor, but I've always wanted to do one of those American Express television commercials, the ones they build around celebrities. My agents advise me that there has been no reply, although the request was put in five years ago. I presume my image is not exactly what they're looking for to put over any additional sales." He was bemused.

As we walked through the gray city and the rain, Tennessee indicated the theatre where *Sugar Babies* was playing to packed houses. The sign was three stories high. "That's what they want now, baby. That's the ticket. Though I wouldn't give a dime to spend a minute with Mickey Rooney and Ann Miller, all the rest of America would. It makes my chances look pretty slim, pretty slim."

As we neared our destination, a young woman rushed up to him. "Is it you Mr. Williams?"

"To all appearances, my dear. May I help you with something?"

"Oh, Mr. Williams, my professor says you're the greatest in America. The greatest of this century. I'm writing my thesis on your work . . ."

She went on for at least three minutes, when we broke away.

"You'll notice her professor didn't say the greatest what," said the ironic Mr. Williams.

At Eastman and Eastman, we were greeted with great, if feigned, exuberance. The elder Eastman was a large, Dickensian sort of gentleman, intelligently affable and radiant with concern. "Well, Tennessee, we have a lot of information for you. Do you wish to relax a little first? You look a little tense."

"In that this is my sixty-ninth birthday, which I'm certain is to be among my last, and that I have a play opening on Broadway tonight, would you grant me some legitimate reasons for being what you call tense?"

"Quite right, Tennessee. Quite right," said the elder Mr. Eastman. "Now to business. You're quite a rich man, Tennessee, quite a rich man."

"That information comes at an opportune moment," Tennessee volunteered. "Bruce seems to be convinced I'm about to be tarred and feathered and run out of town on a rail."

"That's an exaggeration, Tennessee. I can only deal with your insights and experience. This is all new to me, gentlemen, and I'm only here to help Tennessee as a friend and in no official capacity," I said, knowing that clarity of role and definition might be of use when dealing with attorneys.

The elder Mr. Eastman raised a Dickensian eyebrow. "Tennessee says you're more than that. However, Tennessee, should we go through your pro forma now?"

"Before that I want to see what my legal position is regarding my brother, Dakin. He's taken to libelling me on live radio, saying I'm hooked on morphine and other heavy drugs. Can I do something legally to shut him up?"

The means by which the Eastmans had risen to eminence in the legal tinderbox of show business law was immediately apparent. They were the least litigious firm I had ever encountered.

"Now, Tennessee," said Eastman, "you must consider your fame. You really are in the public domain and that's the harsh truth in the matter. If a lawsuit would console you, we might venture an exploration, but the outcome, in our experience, would be in doubt from the start. Now, do you wish us to proceed on this matter of your brother, Dakin Williams?"

Tennessee and I both reeled with the calm lucidity of this pronouncement. Thankfully, it settled the matter in the name of family unity or what passed for it in Tennessee's increasingly divisive sibling associations.

The elder Eastman really was an amusing man. When it came time to reveal the details of Tennessee's wealth, he asked Tennessee if I were to be present for the unveiling. Tennessee asked their advice on the matter and they allowed as how there might be details too personal for any but his attorneys to share. Tennessee agreed. As Eastman showed me to the waiting room, he winked in a secretive manner at me. "You just sit here by the door, Bruce. We want you to be close by should anything we have to say prove unsettling to Tennessee."

I had no sooner settled in the leather lounge chair by the door and picked up a copy of *Time,* when I heard Eastman's voice boom through the door. "You're a very rich man, Tennessee. You're worth $11 million!" I gather that's all Eastman assumed I wanted to know, because the discussion was conducted from then on in a normal tone of voice, which spared me the details, except on a few occasions when Tennessee must have wanted me to share in something, for then his voice would boom, "If I can't sue Dakin, I can at least disinherit him, can't I?" The great Eastman voice boomed its reply: "I wouldn't disinherit him entirely, Tennessee. It could delay the settlement of your estate, which time we all, of course, hope is far off. Leave him a token sum and he's relatively powerless." "We'll do it that way then," said Tennessee in a large voice. "I suppose I have to leave my mother in the will. She must have made enough on the royalties of *Menagerie* by now to require nothing more from me." Further discussion murmured.

Tennessee emerged shortly thereafter. The elder Eastman, head reared back, bowed in his Dickensian manner from the waist as we departed.

"Perhaps not quite as satisfying as an audience with the Pope," said Tennessee, "but fully as meaningful, as I'm certain you'll agree."

CHAPTER XI

Days of Justice Continue

DESPITE THE GOOD NEWS from his attorneys (if, indeed, it was news) Tennessee was clearly morose and, as he said, thirsty. We stopped for a glass of wine at the Plaza Oak Bar and discussed the possibilities.

As the incessant drizzle shrouded the park across the way, Tennessee began to muse on the best ways to pass the time before we all reconnoitered at the Voglis apartment before the entourage set out for the opening and the birthday party, which I was determined, for Tennessee's sake, to short circuit.

Of all the many utterances one might have conjectured would come next from the playwright on his day of reckoning, his was truly laughable in its context.

"I wonder if Maria has anything decent to wear tonight. I think our next step is to shop Third Avenue and buy her a suitable outfit."

"Are we speaking of the Lady St. Just who lives, accord-

ing to her own words, in a palace on Gerald Road in
London? I think, Tennessee, that she will have come prepared."

"She thinks she's prepared, but often she is not. We'll
drop this damned manuscript off at the *Times* and then head
for the shops."

We did that, holding the taxi in the rain as the opening
night Tennessee Williams editorial was left at the reception
desk for editorial evaluation.

"From what you've said of the editorial position of the
New York Times vis a vis you Tennessee, is it really worth
bothering to submit anything to them?"

"Of course, it's a wasted effort. But it's an effort I must
make. I must do everything I can for the play."

With lethargy borne of fatigue, we proceeded to shop for
Maria. This was total madness, I thought, but at least it
wasn't physically self-destructive, as his other activities of
choice might have proved to be. At last, he found just the
garment he wanted for her. Even this encounter was not to
be free from what Tennessee often called "the Manhattan
sense of mirth."

When the shop girl announced that the store did not
accept American Express, Tennessee pulled out his check-
book, which, in the manner of celebrities, was simply
imprinted "Tennessee Williams," with no address. The girl
demurred at accepting the check. "Do you know who
Tennessee Williams is?" I said, rather too grandly for the
occasion, but frustration drives each of us to less than
optimal social acts. "I know the name," she allowed, "but
he doesn't look anything like his pictures."

"Thank God for that," said Tennessee. "Now, here's the
check. Hurry. We're late for an engagement." The innate
authority in his voice carried the day, at least in this matter.

It was only 4:00 P.M. The party was at six. "We'll go see

the Nijinsky film with Alan Bates. I hear he's good in the part of Diaghilev," said Tennessee.

Throughout the film, Tennessee carried on a wildly amusing running commentary. Though our fellow film-goers were less than amused by our chuckles and roars, it was a very helpful, therapeutic session.

"Do you think they got that skunk's stripe of white just right?" said Tennessee, regarding Diaghilev's famous tonsorial trademark. True to character, Alan Bates held a handkerchief to his face during almost all human encounters. "That's good," said Tennessee. "At least they knew he was a hypochondriacal diabetic, terrified of catching anything communicable. I imagine poor Nijinski must have found it disconcerting, as he did so much else, when Diaghilev made love to him with a white hankie covering half his face [hearty chuckle]."

As we left the Loews Theatre, I said, "If that's the way you see movies, I'm glad we didn't go to see *Caligula* (which was just up the street)."

He laughed. "Maybe we'll do that some other time, although I hear it's terrible, beyond redemption, you know."

Now, the evening's onslaught could no longer be delayed.

"We'll walk to Voglis's," said Tennessee.

"But, Tennessee, that's twenty-five blocks away," I said.

"If we did that," said Tennessee, "we might be suitably tempted to just go on walking, baby. All right, let's get a conveyance."

We arrived at an apartment empty of all save Maria. At first glance, she would not need the smart Chanel suit Tennessee had bought for her. She was in a commanding, floor-length, rather operatic gown. "At least you got him here," she said. "Tennessee, we're going to keep this simple. I've bought a big brie and we'll just put that on the table. What do you think?"

Of all things Tennessee was thinking, it was not of cheese. "You might consult with Bruce," he said. "He knows how to throw a party correctly. We had a lovely party at Maxim's in Chicago when *Clothes* opened there. Bruce, what do you think of Maria's brie?" he said, fully maliciously.

"Now there you are, Tennessee. I've caught you at it, which will make it simpler to explain things to Bruce. Tennessee loves to set people against each other and then step back and watch the action. I'm certain he's told you all sorts of terrible things about me and for all you know, he's told me things about you which would make me dislike you. But it doesn't matter." Here, she rose back in a regal attitude and pronounced: "We don't move in the same circles and it's fully doubtful that we'll ever see each other again, so it doesn't matter what Tennessee's said."

"There's a rather noticeable omission here," said Tennessee.

"I told you I want to keep the party simple," said Maria.

"Well, you're not going to keep it this simple, Maria," he said, darkly. "Bruce, kindly find the Voglis's wine cellar. I'm thirsty."

Maria shouted, "All you can think of is drink and after all I've done for you!"

"From the way you speak, you'll give Bruce the mistaken impression that we've been married fifty years. Providence has spared me that fate. Now, Maria, be good and simply open the wine. We wish to freshen up."

Tennessee went into the bath first. He took a little longer than seemed appropriate. "What are you doing in there, Tennessee? That was a long movie. I've got to take a piss."

"Come on in, baby. I won't do anything to bother you."
And there were the needles again. He had evidently
pocketed some from the morning.
"I hate that, Tennessee. I can't be around it. I'm going
to check into the hotel. I'll come back for you to take you to
the theatre. I hope you're still alive when I return."
He looked terribly hurt and angry, simultaneously.
"Well, you got me this far, which is further than I thought
I'd get." He hesitated with his injection preparations.
"Couldn't we just get through this on wine, Tennessee?
Couldn't we try to do that?"
"You don't know the pain I'm in," he said.
"Don't insult me, Tennessee. Why do you think I came
at all? Of course I know what you're going through."
He began to look at the syringe and needle in the palm
of his hand rather helplessly.
"If you'll give me that stuff, I'll get you a glass of wine,"
I said. To my intense relief, he handed over the parapher-
nalia. "Why don't you lie down for a while, Tennessee?
There's a nice dark bedroom just outside this door. I'll go
get you a glass of good red wine." He complied.
I went to the kitchen and fetched the wine. "He's not
going to go cold turkey tonight, Maria," I said. "And if he's
going to get a little chemical relief, I'd rather he found it in
wine." I tossed the junk Tennessee handed me into the
wastebasket.
"He'll hate you for this, one day," said Maria. "You don't
know him."
"But I do know him, Maria. I'm trusting to his better
side, which I've tried to sustain ever since I met him. I've
had a lot of practice. I had an alcoholic father."
I brought the wine to Tennessee, who had retired to the
bedroom. He sipped a little of the wine and held my hand
for a few minutes. "You will take me away, won't you,

Bruce? Remember what I said last night. If things go
wrong, we get on a jet and fly away. We flee this city!"
    "I'm going to get us rooms at the Alrae. I'll go get our
bags at the apartment and I'll call the travel agent from the
hotel. That's just in case, Tennessee. Who knows? We did
pretty well in Chicago. We might fare as well here." It was
as much of a pep talk as I could rally.
    I returned an hour later, having completed my mission
in attaining hotel accommodations and setting up contingency travel plans. Tennessee's agent, who seemed to know
her ground very well, said she'd see about a red-eye special
to Miami and Key West. Tennessee had talked of going
directly to Sicily, but I thought that a rather problematical
choice as an immediate destination.
    Upon entering the Voglis apartment, I was the dis-
pleased cynosure of all eyes. The party for the opening had
foregathered during my absence and a new cast of people
were now on stage, many of them familiar to me from the
pages of Tennessee's *Memoirs*. Among them: Kate Muldaur,
or "Texas Kate" as he called her, and Henry McIlhenny, the
great Philadelphia art collector and friend of such twentieth century luminaries as Samuel Barber and, of course,
Tennessee.
    They all turned to greet me. Henry McIlhenny was a
great, plum-colored gentleman of immaculate grooming
and attire. "I headed up a great contingent of limousines
today just for Tennessee's opening," he said, rather grandly.
I noticed that his entourage included a bevy of aston-
ishingly beautiful young men, all dressed in some twentieth century version of an eighteenth century court
costume. They were all in varying hues of velvet suitings.
Tennessee gave me one of his conspiratorial smiles as I took
in the scene. He kindly went himself to the drinks table,
now commandeered by the host himself, and made me a

J & B and soda. "We should stay here for a bit more," he whispered. "After all they've all gone to a great deal of trouble to get here, though God knows why. And Henry with that funereal cortege of his from Philadelphia!"

I sat down with my drink and immediately Texas Kate jumped into my lap. "You're different from the usual Tennessee people," she said.

"So are you. At least you have an open spontaneity about you," I said, adjusting myself to her intimate company.

"You've seen the play. What do you think of it?" she asked. "At this point," I said, "I think the play and the activity surrounding it have merged into one event. There is so much going on tonight that I hope Tennessee can get through it."

"If I can give you some quick advice," she said, "do what you discussed doing before all this chaos started up." Obviously, Tennessee had filled her in on what our plans were, or so at least I thought.

Tennessee came up to us. "May I borrow my partner in crime, here," he said.

We went into the bedroom. "In case you're thinking the worst, you're right. I just thought I'd tell you that. You know they brought those pretty boys here in order for me to take my pick. While you were away, Maria opined that any one of them would be willing to accompany me to Sicily. They're handpicked and, no doubt, 'hand drilled,' to extend some kind of authority over me while I'm out of their sight. But they have utterly failed in their mission and for a very obvious reason. Not one of them is my type. I can't stand fancy boys all dressed up like that. I'm forced to conclude that Maria doesn't know me at all. They can all go back to London with Maria and try their luck there, although Henry has his eye on one or two of them. I wonder if they'll like the confines of Philadelphia as an alternative [chuckle]."

"Can you imagine all the trouble they've gone to set this up, Tennessee? Just think if they turned their time to something useful."

"I think this century has had enough of fascism, don't you? Let's be glad that they busy themselves in this rather harmless way."

"Where are your celebrated goddaughters, Tennessee? Maria's been raving about their extensive modelling assignments."

"Appropriately, still dressing. You've been assigned to squire them to the theatre. I know you don't want to have anything to do with Maria, but I'd appreciate it if you'd do this for me."

When we returned to the living room, Maria's daughters had presented themselves. Somehow, in transit, the hems of their floor-length gowns had become undone and Maria was busy trying to pin them up.

"As soon as you're done, Maria, I think we should proceed to the theatre. Bruce has agreed to take my godchildren in a cab. We'll all meet in the lobby of the Cort Theatre and get our seat assignments there. Milton has arranged our boxes for us."

Two of the male hookers joined us in the cab, so, knowing what I did, I could think of nothing polite to say. We travelled in perfect silence to the theatre.

CHAPTER XII

---❧---

Blind Justice

PACING ON THE STREET just before the entrance to the
Cort lobby was the play's director, José Quintero. Wildly
disheveled and wet, his black leather trench coat askew, he
was in no mood to give any further direction. I asked him if
he had seen Tennessee. "He's in there somewhere, God-
damn it!" Tennessee had been initially swept up in the
celebrity audience, but had soon, with some diffidence,
moved on to his box. I fought my way through the crowd
and joined him there.

"A good turnout, anyway," he said. Maria, with her
coterie of daughters and call boys in the box behind us,
formed a kind of Greek choral unit to the drama unfolding
before us. "Ten, there's Milton! And he's with Claudette
Colbert! Ten, there's Maureen. I knew she'd make it. Milton reminded her it was your birthday. She came even
though you didn't speak with her yesterday!" Maria was in
heaven.

"Maria evidently feels that I'm blind as well as mentally incompetent," he said in an aside to me. "It's after the appointed time. Let's just dim the lights and get this over with as gracefully as possible."

Eyes followed fingers to the box above their heads. The great playwright had been spotted and was now pointed out to all. Tennessee tried to ignore it. In these situations he was truly uneasy and shy, despite the fact that he said that he had given up shyness as a present to himself on his twenty-first birthday.

The lights dimmed. The curtain rose. All our hopes could not dispel the wrongness of Kenneth Haigh as Scott. And he, having long ago been informed of the playwright's displeasure, seemed to add belligerence to his concept of the role of Scott.

"He's more wooden than ever," said Tennessee in a whisper. "No one would believe he had ever even sampled liquor let alone downed a fifth a day. We have Maria to thank for him, you know. It's her and her British theatrical connections that we have to thank for this."

I replied: "I'd heard he'd died and gone to Yale."

It gave us both some pleasure to carry on this surreptitious conversation with Maria sitting right behind us. She was volubly explaining who Scott and Zelda were to her charges, which freed us for our discourse. The play played on before us.

The scene with Geraldine Page practicing her ballet at the bar brought evident strain to the audience. I could sense Tennessee tightening. "She does look all wrong for the part. Maybe they'll believe the insulin. And you can't hear anything she says. There's now more mystery to the proceedings than I had allowed for, initially," he said, chuckling morosely.

Clothes for a Summer Hotel as written and staged was a

departure in form from Tennessee's great, earlier plays. Here he had abandoned the Aristotelian mode of continuity of time and place. There is a party scene in which many representatives of the Lost Generation gather. Tennessee uses this format as the means for passing on anecdotage about the participants who had entered common mythology about the era. Hemingway was there, and there was a cameo appearance by Mrs. Patrick Campbell, the aged actress who lived on and out of her own age. Her anecdote, which was no surprise to anyone familiar with the literature of the period, brought a muted gasp from the audience.

"I can't even get away with a feisty old broad, anymore, it would seem," he whispered.

One of the scenes which most caused the audience to writhe in its collective seats was the beach scene, where Zelda flirts with infidelity with a French aviator of great romantic—and physical—appeal. The sight of Geraldine Page, twice the age of her partner and half again as heavy, made the trite image of the Wagnerian soprano seem more acceptable to romance.

"What's happened to Gerry?" mused Tennessee. "She was so lovely in *Summer and Smoke*. She was believable in *Bird*. Age is so cruel to us. She should just stop. Of course, she'd never accept the character roles to which she is now more appropriate."

Intermission came with a dash to the lobby to meet old acquaintances. I remained in the box. A weary Tennessee returned with the information that he had met with someone who had once made a film depicting his origins in the South combined with interviews attempting to catch his present-day state of mind.

"A dear old thing really. Harmless. The film he's made is rather touching. Maybe we should ask Harry [Rasky] for a

print. If we balanced that with Tallulah's uncut version of
Lifeboat we'd really have something approaching the truth
of the matter!"

The curtain rose on *Clothes* and the actors' action seemed
stepped up a pace, as though everyone wanted to get
through it and on to the real action of the night—waiting
for the notices or attending the poorly-conceived combination sixty-ninth birthday party/cast party at an upper East
Side restaurant. "Many ghosts are sure to appear there,"
said Tennessee, "myself among them."

When *Clothes* had played in Chicago, there was still
hope in the air and the performers gave of themselves
sufficiently to carry the play, even with the said miscasting
of the two central roles. Here, a sense of doom precluded
any enthusiasm from the cast. And the audience was disori-
ented by the play of time which Tennessee had thought
essential to the realization of character within the scope of
the play's ghostly action. If any in the audience had stopped
to read the stagebill before seeing the play, they would have
been helped along by Tennessee's apologia, which was
printed in the program: "This is a ghost play. Of course in a
sense all plays are ghost plays, since players are not actually
whom they play. Our reason for taking extraordinary license with time and place is that in an asylum and on its
grounds liberties of this kind are quite prevalent; and also
these liberties allow us to explore in more depth what we
believe is truth of character. And so we ask you to indulge
us with the licenses we take for a purpose which we consider quite earnest."

But very few in the audience, particularly theatre professionals and critics, were going to grant Tennessee that
license. If *Clothes for a Summer Hotel* had emerged on the
stage with the dramatic coherence of *Cat on a Hot Tin Roof*
or even the somewhat disputed *Night of the Iguana,* this

group might have granted him renewed status of a contemporary kind among them. But this was a play—it was obvious to all—which still needed work of a substantial kind: rewriting, editing, refocusing, and even recasting.

As the curtain came down, there was uncertainty as to whether the play was actually over. There was a painful moment before applause began. Tennessee shifted painfully in his seat and rose, as if to go. At that moment a stage manager appeared in the spotlight before the curtain and announced that the playwright was in the audience and asked that the group applaud him on his sixty-ninth birthday. The audience rose and turned to the box. For a moment, Tennessee seemed to think the applause was for someone else, but then he graciously stood, assuming a somewhat retiring stance, and lifted his arms and open palms in a quiet expression of acceptance. Never one to milk a moment, Tennessee prodded my arm and we hurried from the box, down the stairs, and out into the alley through the stage door.

Because of the stage door alley's natural shade and the constant drizzle, we did not take in the gray hoards which formed wakes to either side. We were first aware of the crowd when one man emerged from the shadows with at least a dozen hardbound Tennessee Williams books in his arms. "Happy Birthday, Mr. Williams," he said. "Would you be kind enough to autograph these for me?" The imposition seemed incredible to me under the pressure of the circumstances, but Tennessee obliged, in a very courtly and affable manner. "Of course, my friend," he said and silently went on autographing the twelve volumes. Others importuned him as we moved through the hundreds of people, who, unable to get into the theatre for financial or booking reasons, had gathered in the alley and all the way down one full block. He obliged each of them.

"These are my people," he said, quietly. "I know these are my readers, people with whom I've communicated in some quite human and genuine manner. That man who wanted me to sign all those books, I know he'll have to sell them, probably to pay his rent. These are the people I relate to and for. They're all so far removed from the group inside the theatre. And to think that some one critic in there is going to decide against their being able to see one last big play of mine. I could feel it as we sat there during the performance of my play. They're warming for the kill, baby, they're warming for the kill."

It was an immensely moving experience to see the spontaneous warmth and appreciation of the crowds massed on the streets as we walked from the theatre. There was a warm wave of gentle applause as he reached each group. Surely, I thought this display of honest response to him must do much to dispel the rising tide of rejection which now seemed imminent.

"Let's have a drink before we face the music," he said. I was happy to think we would have some time together to discuss the travel arrangements he had urged me to make. I was determined to support the plan he had made the night before, which seemed derived from long experience and so, ultimately sensible. To go back immediately to what was most important to him, his writing. And to do that before the body blows of critical rejection depleted him of whatever self-esteem he retained.

It seemed to help him that we went into a restaurant that knew nothing of the night's events and where we would relax in anonymity. Since the wine he now preferred was available, he ordered a full bottle. Despite the fact that the cast and press were assembling at the same time for his birthday celebration, he required this time away from it all to regroup. It obviously helped to have some supportive companionship while he did so.

"Tennessee, I don't suppose it would be good for business to avoid the birthday party with the press and cast, but we could slip away after you've made an appearance. Your agent has you on a late flight to Miami with a good connection to Key West."

"Am I going back alone, then?" he asked.

"I thought it might be better for you to just go home and rest. Jim can meet you and take care of the details."

Very wearily, he said, "Can't you take me down? Are your engagements and commitments so pressing?"

"I'll take you to Key West if we leave after your appearance at the birthday party and before you further victimize yourself by appearing at Maria's party afterward. If the reviews are bad, will you be comforted by having the circus atmosphere party around you? I took you at your word the other night. Our conversation brought into focus my role, at least for now, with you. I can help you through this thing. I can help you exercise your survival mechanisms."

"You really think the reviews will warrant that I flee here?"

"Call it a sixth sense, backed up by what I sensed in the audience tonight and by the truly vicious people you have had representing you here in New York. You've been thrown to the lions. I know now, without question, that you were right in your Key West assessment. The theatre world does want you out of the way. They don't like it that you're not cooperating as they expect. I've come to think that this New York opening is kind of a planned coup de grace for you. Why sit around and be made a fool of?"

"Waiter, I can't possibly finish this full bottle of wine. May I carry it with me? I feel I may need it as the night proceeds." The waiter, oddly I thought, wrapped the bottle in aluminum foil and gave it to Tennessee. "How far is it to our party?" he looked up at me and cackled.

"At least ten blocks, Tennessee."

"We'll walk it, then. The television notices will be on by the time we get there. If they're as bad as you seem to think they'll be, we'll take those tickets and get on a jet plane to Key West."

I now noticed a shift in Tennessee's perceptions. I was becoming a kind of catalyst of the bad news that seemed to be pervading the New York experience. I had been aware of these mood shifts from the beginning, but I felt a commitment to help him through this bad time as best I could, even if it meant becoming an object for his somewhat blurred, but nonetheless agonizing, sense of rejection.

The relentless drizzle continued, a metaphor Manhattan could not resist offering up to us. As we walked down Madison Avenue, a popular interpreter of Cole Porter, whom I had known for years, saw us coming and was so unsettled by our appearance together that the sheet music he carried was blown away in the rainy wind, in a great flurry of white wings. Tennessee scarcely noticed. The aluminum foil wrapped wine bottle glowed in his grasp, reflecting wet city light, a type—again—of symbolic lantern for him.

By the time we arrived at the party, late, the group had assembled for, as Tennessee said, no less than a "gallows hanging." Pat Lawford and Oliver Smith, the set designer, were posed in a New York partyish way, their chat ceasing as they saw Tennessee's wet arrival. It was the darkest restaurant in Manhattan and we were both glad of that, but only for a moment. We soon realized that the lights had been dimmed to allow us all to view the television reviews. They were just coming up as we arrived.

"I must take this opportunity, before the death sentence is passed down, to thank everyone who helped with the play," he said.

Accordingly, we went up to the set designer, Oliver

Smith. Either he had moved on to new heights of pretentious stuffiness or had come to suffer from the catatonia which seemed to inform the mood of the gathering. "I'm so pleased you and your friend here liked my designs, Tennessee," he said with grand hauteur.

"But that isn't exactly what we said, you know. I believe I thanked you for your work. Bruce here thought your 'burning bush' motif a bit heavy-handed in the first act and I'm not certain he was alone in that judgment. But, again, thank you for your work."

I now realized that this was to be his catechism of pledged gratitude, as he had outlined in his ideal plan of action for play openings. We accordingly went to find José Quintero, the director, who now huddled in a dark corner, alone except for his friend.

"No doubt this will be what is so elegantly described as a swan song for both of us, José," said Tennessee. "They won't want us back again. But then, they didn't want us this time, did they? I wished to thank you for what must have come to seem a truly heroic effort, José."

The men's room was a labyrinth away from the party room, and as I moved through its corridors, obligingly set up with television monitors at a convenient interval of perhaps twenty feet, I couldn't miss the voice of electronic doom as I went off to the washroom. Returning, the TV reviewers were concluding their ax work. There was nothing subtle about it at all. The play was doomed, Tennessee's return to Broadway an ill-advised disaster.

I returned to the party room for a scene perfect in its mockery of fate. The cast had gathered around a huge, inelegant sheet cake and, there, not with a pastry knife as called for in most cake-cutting ceremonies, but a butcher knife, a tipsy Maureen Stapleton assayed her duties as chief birthday celebrant. Tennessee, who was beside her at the cake table, looked up at me with still a trace of amusement at this bizarre scene. The play was dead, the birthday party went on. With a look of true displeasure at Tennessee, Maureen stabbed the vast cake with appropriate savagery. Then, with the obligato of the TV news in the background, the group assembled and actually sang "Happy Birthday" to Tennessee.

I grabbed our coats and took Tennessee firmly by the arm and guided him to the door. He was truly as near to clinical catatonia as I had ever seen him, but he came along. We began to walk up the street.

"Let's just get a cab to the hotel, collect our things, and go out to La Guardia, Tennessee. This is playing out just as we thought. I can't bear to see you surrounded by all this insensitivity."

"We must go to Maria's party first. She went to a lot of work, you know. They'll be expecting us."

"She bought a brie. Are you really in a party mood, Tennessee?"

Words were clearly beginning to fail him and he now found it difficult to talk.

"Tennessee, I know you put together your escape plan in a more calm moment for implementation when you wouldn't be at your best. It was a good idea. Let's use it. Let's just go to Key West."

He just put one foot ahead of the other and shuffled through the rain.

When we arrived at the party, Maria and her daughters were busily passing out crackers with brie. Elia Kazan, whom Tennessee loved as his truest interpreter, stood, rather ghostly in gray, in the center of the room. He's a man, like Tennessee, of small physical stature but of strong and reassuring presence. His look of immense sympathy brought a glimpse of sanity to the proceedings. He bowed in a courtly manner as Tennessee came into the room.

Tennessee disappeared into the bathroom. One of the call boys came up to me and said, "We've got some uppers for him back there."

He had either injected a significant dose of amphetamines or swallowed a handful, because the Tennessee who returned to the living room wore an entirely different demeanor. He had removed his suit jacket, rolled up his sleeves, and loosened his tie. He looked like a scrappy little barroom fighter. Although he tried to look tough, he was weaving on his feet. He made an inclusive gesture with his arms.

He weaved back to me. "Sit down, you. Everybody sit down. I know what's going on here." Turning to me he shouted in a rage, "I know you wanted this play to fail. Now sit down with the rest of them."

I remained standing. The impact of his words prompted only one reaction: survival. I shook my head slightly, got my coat, and left. And though the insights of an educated life worked to rationalize the incident through considerations of the deadly mix of drugs and adrenaline, I was enraged. I'd stay in New York through the morning, to see what it brought. But unless it brought something like the true Tennessee I had come to know, I was going back to Chicago and, once I had calmed down, write it all down to experience.

How distant all this seemed to that moment of redemption just a few evenings ago, when, in a sudden gesture which was a moment's recreation of Michelangelo's famous Sistine scene, Tennessee reached out his hand and touched mine. As we stood on the balcony overlooking Manhattan in the definitive crepuscular twilight, the liberating energy that suddenly sprang from his touch seemed to bring up all the lights which were, at just that moment, brightening the citys gathering dark.

Tennessee's detested T.S. Eliot seemed now to mock:

"We all go into the dark." And now it seemed almost certain that Tennessee was cooperating fully with those who would usher him there.

And so it was that Tennessee's sixty-ninth birthday came to a close. It was March 26, 1980.

In early 1980, Tennessee had been taking care of himself in preparation for the rigors of Broadway play production. Here he is in a rather brisk arrival at Maxim's de Paris for a party in his honor. (credit, Pintozzi © 1980)

Page by Page. Tenessee examines one of the many orders received by dance legend Ruth Page (right) at Maxim's. As for Geraldine, Tennessee had already come to think that a reference to insulin in *Clothes for a Summer Hotel* might account for her puffiness, which was clearly occasioned by other pursuits. (credit, Pintozzi © 1980)

Tennessee was taken instantly by the charms of Maxim's de Paris owner Nancy Goldberg. After this photograph, Geraldine was never to smile again, at least for the run of *Clothes*. (credit, Pintozzi © 1980)

The production of Tennessee's last big play was doomed the moment he relinquished his original title. Certainly, as dramatically illustrated here, *Some Problems for the Moose Lodge* more aptly underscored the "tragic irony" for which the playwright was aiming than the lame creation of his then menage-in-residence, *A House Not Meant to Stand*. This was only a slight improvement of the much encouraged *House of Papier Mache*, offered by the same friend who had suggested Tennessee listen to *Jonathan Livingston Seagull* in order to secure a more contemporary grasp on the national mind-set. In any event, the play went down to total critical defeat.

In the production of *A House Not Meant to Stand*, Charlie was played by Scott Jaeck of whom the playwright opined: "He's got the raw energy combined with the true sensitivity of the young Brando." Peg Murray (right, as Bella) was brought in for the mainstage production of *House* because of her talismanic position in the playwright's pantheon of play-saviors. She had been brought in toward the end of the mid-70's run of *Small Craft Warnings* in order to shore up its rapidly sinking box office. (credit, Goodman Theatre, Chicago)

A shared moment of the good humor that was hard to come by during the 1981 rehearsals of the Goodman's studio production *A House Not Meant to Stand*. Gregory Mosher (right), then artistic director of the Goodman, was "always fighting the good fight," according to Tennessee. Mosher had to contend with the mercurial playwright, the Goodman Board of Directors, and the unbalanced direction of the play. (credit, Goodman, Theatre, Chicago)

This shot is pure Tennessee Williams dramaturgy. A freelance photographer for a national weekly magazine discovered him in a bar at the Drake Hotel and prepared to take a shot of him there. "Surely," said the playwright, "there are more appropriate and recognizable landmarks with which we can verify my presence here in Chicago than this poorly illuminated bar." Accordingly, dressed only for a summer hotel, he ventured out onto the North Avenue beach of Lake Michigan for this "winter of cities" photograph. (credit, Goodman Theatre, Chicago)

By 1982, Mosher had managed to provide Tennessee with a main-stage production of *A House Not Meant to Stand*, although the lack of elbow room was evident as shown here during rehearsals for the 1981 studio production of the play. The cast was happy and creative when the playwright was with them, aimless and unhappy in the directorial vacuum of his absence. (credit, Goodman Theatre, Chicago)

CHAPTER XIII

The Crystal Crocodile

THE ALRAE'S DESK MANAGER called me at ten the next morning to inform me that, as of tomorrow, I was no longer a guest of Mr. Williams. I allowed to how I was moving on to more congenial climes in any event and thanked the manager for the courtesy of his call. If I stayed, I assumed my American Express card would be as good as his.

My call to Tennessee's room went unanswered. A call to the desk elicited the information that Mr. Williams did not wish to be disturbed. I had wanted to see Tennessee in the clarity of the morning, before I left for Chicago, but I began to pack under the assumption that I would not be able to do so. Maria now had him firmly in her charge and it would be difficult to extricate him, or so I thought.

Later there was an improbable, though somewhat reassuring, note awaiting me. Its message was:

Dear Bruce: You deserve an island in the sun as reward for your fortitude and patience during these days of Justice.

Rather than join you in Key West with the Lady St. Just, I have opted to take her to San Juan where, at the Caribe Hilton, there are the therapeutic sea water pools filled twice daily by tides. Have a good evening. I know you understand why Maria may not join us in Key West. But I do hope you will join me for dinner at Voglis's should you wish to . . . we'll be there about 7:30. Love, "1O."

Pleased by the rational tone of the note, I continued to try to reach Tennessee, but had no response. Clearly, his vitriolic performance of the night before had been brought on by the tension of the opening, fueled by the drugs. But, despite the warming mood of the note, I had no interest now in a trip to Key West, with Maria orchestrating Tennessee's mood as he tried to recover in the therapeutic pool of San Juan's Caribe Hilton. I left a note for him stating my travel arrangements and saying we would be in touch once the air had cleared. But I had no real intention of ever seeing him again.

To affirm my design, I had as a symbol the opening night gift Tennessee had received from a New Orleans director of his plays. It was a crystal crocodile. The accompanying note had read, "To the greatest crocodile of them all."

It is not only easy to turn your back on a crocodile. It is the only sensible thing to do.

ENTR'ACTE

———————⌒◆⌒———————

"YOU LAUGH IN YOUR sleep, you know," Tennessee commented one morning as he woke me for a morning chat. "You are an original. I've never known anyone to do that before."

Alas laughter, even in sleep, could no longer accompany the gallows humor of recent events. Word of Tennessee's sad, tiger-like ragings on Broadway reached me in Chicago.

The flickering television reviews had the advantage of being evanescent. Those in print would lay about for agonized perusal, providing enough psychic salt for Broadway wounds to last Tennessee the rest of his life.

The reviews offered a universal condemnation. They formed a sad, long litany of reference to fading powers; inappropriate and ineptly grasped material; ghastly casting. In the last, at least, Tennessee and I were confirmed in our judgment. Gerry and Kenneth Haigh had proved too much a burden for the gossamer web of words Tennessee

had offered up to the mob. One critic, who evidently knew
no restraint, referred to Geraldine Page's face as "having a
mouth like a cut purse." Though the play was down for the
count, Tennessee summoned the energy for a last, demeaning fight.

When I heard from Jim what Tennessee proposed, I
tried to reach him by phone. Maria St. Just had shut down
all access to Tennessee by phone, so I resorted to a telegram, trusting that the implied urgency might get my
message to Garcia: "If you try to keep *Clothes* alive with
your private funds, you will be using artificial means to
continue its life. It won't be considered a heroic gesture,
which I do, but as a thoroughly ill-advised venture by a
man no longer in control of himself or his actions."

And so it proved all too painfully to be. Tennessee went
upon the stage during a matinee and made a short speech in
a garrulous and weaving fashion. He said truly that a play
into which a playwright of some accomplishment had put a
great deal of work and into which many talented people
had contributed their time and energy, deserved a longer
stay. The critics, who were, after all, only subjective indi-
viduals, should not have the last word. The play should
speak for itself. He pledged $20 thousand of his own funds
to keep the play open for an additional week in the hope
that word of mouth would extend its life. The audience,
conditioned by the media for more than a decade, reacted
mostly with confusion. Some felt only simple regret for the
great playwright's sad plight.

The gesture produced some copy for the press, which
was bad for Tennessee and worse for the play. The gesture
insured that the play limped to a last, sad closing rather
than just stopped quickly as destiny seemed to demand.
"Couldn't the son of a bitch at least let us get out quick,"
Ms. Page was heard to say at a cast lunch one day.

Now, with all traces of dignity erased with consummate skill, Tennessee was at last prepared for the now ignominious flight to Key West. The price of this delayed departure was that the Caribe Hilton and its thermal, tidal pools were no longer in the scenario. The terrace at Pier House in Key West would have to do.

According to Tennessee's cousins, Jim and Stell Adams, Maria was in firm control of mission Key West. Tennessee himself was, in Stell's words, "a basket case." Jim Adams, who had seemed so boundlessly graced with energy, was in a state of advanced depression as well. In phone calls to me in Chicago, the sad tale began to unfold.

Jim informed me that Tennessee had invited Gary Tucker and his bait, Schuyler Wyatt, down to Key West after the Chicago run, embroidering the invitations with vague promises of financial support. "Of course," said Jim, "Tom's promises were never fulfilled. He did put them up for two nights at La Terrazza de Marti (a Key West guest house), but then put them out on their own. They really had to scramble for work in order to put a roof over their heads and some food on the table."

I wondered what had gone awry with Gary's plans to advance his own theatrical ambitions. "Tom was just too shot to care about love or even sex when he was down here between Chicago and New York. And then your presence in the mix didn't help Gary's cause either. He had taken to heart your displeasure at their machinations and seemed to be using you as a reality tester for him. Gary and Schuyler were in a true state of alarm down here. Literally at the end of the earth and without a penny to buy their way out."

"I'm on another hit list, apparently," I said from Chicago. "I can just add Gary and Schuy to the lists which were begun by Geraldine Page. And how is the sainted

Maria doing? If I'm testing Tennessee's reality, how does
she escape unscathed?"

"Since Tom's mother, Edwina, has been ill and in decline, we think that Maria is a kind of incarnation of her. A
more active, destructive mother. You know what she did to
Rose—lobotomizing her when that technique was still
highly in question. Unconsciously, Tom is scared shitless
that some woman is going to perform a prefrontal lobot-
omy on him. Of course, I think that might be unnecessary
at this point. Drugs and booze have done a pretty good job
all by themselves."

"I wonder if Maria is acting knowingly in this way. Is she
that shrewd?"

"Just consider her recent past," said Jim. "She comes
fully equipped for the role."

"It enrages me that she keeps getting away with it. Of
course, she sees to it that Tennessee is surrounded only by
the disenfranchised so that she remains in control. She
didn't like it that I worked in the real world and had
contacts who could find her out. She worked overtime in
New York trying to discredit me to Tennessee."

"But that didn't work," said Jim. "He still says 'Bruce
said this, or Bruce would know better about that' to her. Of
course, this turns her purple, which, of course, Tennessee,
even in his current befuddlement, loves. He hasn't lost his
humor or his consciousness completely. At dinner the other
night, Tom brought up your name and Maria became very
huffy, very nervous. She began playing with her gold
chains. Tennessee said, 'Maria, the way you're going at
those gold beads, you'd think you want me to notice them
and add to the collection. Is that at all probable, in your
estimation?' Of course, Maria looked bleak at this and
hurried us all through dinner. She doesn't like her number
called, especially in so public a place as the Casa Marina in

Key West." I was delighted to hear that there was some of the old Tennessee that I loved still in operation.

Jim's sister, Stell, got on the line. "We've never met, but I think we'll be pals. You probably don't want to come down here just now to witness all this mess, but come on down when the waters have cleared. Jim says you're the only one holding things together and, of course, I know Tennessee well enough to know he doesn't appreciate it a damn. But don't let that get in your way. Where there's life there's hope."

I held out small hope that Tennessee might regain the healthy state he had worked so diligently to procure at the time I first met him, which was now only some four months before. The decline had been relentless, aided on each and every step by his old associates, and now, the new. The fact that Gary and Schuy were on the island with Tennessee did not auger well. Somehow, I was convinced, they would thrive there and make their move on Tennessee as soon as the opportunity arose. As soon as a window in his paranoia opened even an inch, I knew they'd be in the house on Duncan Street.

And so, indeed, it happened. The next report I had from Key West reported that Jim had been forced out of his role as general factotum and that Gary had weaseled his way in. In a way, this could only be an economic relief to Jim, who was seldom paid the modest $250 per week that Tennessee had promised him in exchange for his services. Jim, in fact, wound up paying for many of the day-to-day expenses Tennessee and Jim incurred in Key West, which rapidly depleted Jim's small reserves. There was a brief reinstatement of payment directly after the New York experience, but that was curtailed by the advent of the Schuyler contingent. Remorseless in their ambitions, they pushed family and true friends right over the cliff of Tennessee's attentions.

The tale of this *ménage à trois* began with smoke signals
and ended in ruin. This ruin was not a gradual fall, but a
seemless journey of self-abasement through the balance of
Tennessee's theatrical career.

The reports from Key West mingled with the New York
experience caused in me a true rage towards Tennessee. I
suppose that because I had witnessed my father's certain
ruin through alcohol, I was too impatient to witness another truly-gifted person cooperate so fully with the forces
of destruction and then to bear calm witness to the dissolution.

There were symbols from the New York experience and
from the Key West reports which enabled me to form a
defense of my own against all this hellishness and waste. I
began a systematic research of Tennessee's past, outside the
experience of his own *Memoirs*.

Through a journalist friend I had learned of a psychiatrist who had treated Tennessee when he was an intern back
in the early sixties at the time the playwright was in
Chicago for the production of *Night of the Iguana*. Tennessee
had complained of a persistent infection of his ankle. In
fact, he was only able to wear carpet slippers to the theatre
because of the uncomfortable swelling. The doctor, who
was called to the hotel with another M.D. to examine the
patient, found the suite appointed throughout with half-
filled glasses of stale Scotch and the patient abed in a
comatose condition. The doctors carefully examined the
ankle and dressed it. "Williams insisted the wound on his
ankle came from a dog bite, but we both found this
improbable," said the doctor. "The indentations were so
regular and the flesh so symmetrically cleaned from the
bone that we concluded that the wound was inflicted in a
conscious and purposeful manner." I hesitantly fancied that
the doctor was making an allusion to some of the more

arcane practices dramatized in Tennessee's *Suddenly Last
Summer.* In this case, cannibalism. "You and your cohort
really deduced that Tennessee was experimenting with
cannibalism?" "We could come to no other conclusion but
that another human being had actually not only bitten him
but continued to chew. This would also account for the
severity of the infection."

I wondered if his drug intake could possibly bring him
to a pass where he would participate in this kind of mas-
ochistic activity. "Did you determine what particular
drugs he was on at the time?" I asked. "He was mixing an
unbelievable amount of alcohol with Methedrine and other
uppers. And then, to bring himself down, he had several
prescriptions for Seconal, without which he said he
couldn't sleep." I asked what the prognosis was for someone
on this psychogenic mix. "Medically, we could have
brought him off the alcohol and the amphetamines, but
Seconal can be irreversible in its effects. It really scrambles
the brain."

This professional opinion explained the irreversible nature of Tennessee's addiction, in which he had evidently
been abetted by still-practicing physicians throughout the
years. Those whom he had come to for help had only
enabled him to continue his addiction to drugs of an
increasingly lethal nature.

Although it was a professionally-rendered opinion, I
decided to relegate the cannibalism anecdote to the trove of
unverifiable Tennesseeiana with which his career was so
rich. Surely some kinds of human experience should remain untouched. The information on the permanence of
the impact of Seconal was useful in determining just how
Tennessee would ever be if he went back to his pre-*Clothes*
regimen. It was evident in spades that all of his associates,
both past and present, with the exception of myself and a

few good old friends, considered him beyond redemption. But he had quite consciously called to me for a hearing, and I had given my time and my help to him. I was, of course, frustrated that all the good intentions in the world, which we both seemed to have, were not sufficient to bring off the New York episode with more dignity. He should have followed his own good advice and fled to Key West directly from the theatre.

I thought perhaps I could bring him up short with a strong dose of reality, so I sent him an invoice for all the expenses I had incurred in his behalf since he had first come on to Chicago as well as for my time. That act made me feel somewhat better as it put the matter into a professional perspective as opposed to the purely personal. There was no initial response to my angry invoice.

As troubling as was the consideration of the den of thieves into which he had presumably descended in Key West, I armed myself with what I could to dismiss him from serious consideration as a friend.

We were back in Dragon Country—the uninhabitable land that is yet inhabited. And I had seen its flag, the escutcheon a bottle of Seconal intertwined with a crystal crocodile. Under that banner, what hope for him now?

CHAPTER XIV

The Depths Disclose
a Crystal Height

I HAD A BIRTHDAY letter from Tennessee that year. On May 21, 1980, he wrote me a note which was the first word I had from him since New York. The letter read:

"My dear Bruce—It's better to scribble a hopefully legible note on the back of an agent's letter than to maintain this silence any longer. I returned from *Clothes* in nervous shock, from which I've not yet recovered. Hopefully will derive some benefit from a brief vacation in Sicily. I was distressed to hear you weren't feeling well, either, but you look so robust that I feel sure you'll regain health. Rest. Relax in some serene place. I received your invoice and I enclose a check as some payment, which I hope you will accept. I still consider the work you've done for me, as I believe I've said before, a fantastic gesture of sympathy and friendship. Best wishes. Tennessee."

His handwriting was a scrawl of evident pain. His "nervous shock" was evident in the writing itself, the elegant and easy style transformed into a true "scribble." But that scribble was a testament of emotional honesty. And for that reason I prized it and felt the old hope stirring that Tennessee might still come out all right in his fight for what could only be called his existential franchise.

A few weeks after this note, a call came in mid-afternoon from the famous Voglis in New York. "Tennessee is here with me. I want to put him on the phone in a minute, but first I wanted to assure you that Tennessee is much better than we thought. He wants to come to Chicago for a new project. He says you gave him some hope that his work would be accepted there. He wants a reunion with you. Please, as a friend, don't refuse him now. He's coming only to his friends he can trust. But let me give you one piece of advice based on a long friendship: don't do as you evidently did in New York and tell him when the news is bad. Let him find out some other way. I know you did as you thought a good friend would do. But with Tennessee you have to be even a little bit more careful. Now, good luck. Thank you for being his friend. Here he is."

"Bruce, is that you, baby? I didn't know how to get through to you on the phone, you know. Voglis has kindly advised me. I want to come back to Chicago to work on a new venture. I just want to know, if I do come on out there, will you be so kind as to receive me?"

The old spontaneous warmth was still in place. "Of course, Tennessee, I'd love to see you. When are you planning to come?"

"Voglis here will give you the details, which have been written down. I'm looking forward to seeing you. I was uncertain. But now I'll have the chance to explain New York in the calm of some perspective. There are some details to be worked out at Goodman Theatre for the project, but it looks as though it will go through. I'll call just before I depart to let you know I'm on the way."

The tone of Tennessee's voice was wistful, old, sad,

hopeful. In short, irresistible. I couldn't abandon a friend like that, even with the accumulated wisdom of the recent *Clothes* experience. I assumed that there would inevitably be the abrasive mix of entourage involved in his Chicago visit. But I was determined to have little of it and only to see Tennessee apart from whatever group dynamics he may have in mind for the occasion.

When I heard from Voglis that Tennessee's lodging in Chicago would be the Delaware Towers, I deduced that some form of housekeeping was in order. The Delaware Towers specialized in residential accommodations for transients, offering suites of rooms with kitchen facilities. That this was not in the old Tennessee mode was obvious. His earlier requirements were for a pool and prompt room service, both of which were beyond the resources of the Delaware Towers.

"Don't bother meeting me at the airport, baby. I'll just grab a taxi and come on in to town. I'll call you when I get in," he said at the conclusion of a long phone conversation before he left Key West. I assumed he must have something he didn't want me to see at the airport, because airports terrified him. "Crowds in motion paralyze me," he had said the last time I had picked him up at O'Hare. I placed a call to Jim in Key West to see what was up. It was May 21, 1980.

Jim was laughing. "You don't know what he's really up to this time, do you? He's been living with Gary Tucker and Schuyler Wyatt in the Duncan Street house, which he now calls the 'big dormitory.' It's love in bloom for Tennessee. Try not to say there's no fool like an old fool, because it would be only too true. Moved them in and ensconced Schuy—how he loves that name, you know he spells it *Sky* in his heart—as his live-in lover. And suddenly, money's no object. He had Schuy pick out a new convertible, a totally tasteless vehicle, in my opinion. It's silver and a block long. And they go cruising around Key West like Cleopatra on her barge, waving and laughing at the tourists. It's a vulgar display. He's thrown Stell and me out of his house. By the way, I'm surprised to hear from you. Tenn told me you were unwell."

"I think we ought not to let him know we've spoken and just proceed with the evidence at hand. I'm not going to get involved with any of the Tucker proceedings, unless they seem to be getting out of hand and truly harmful to Tennessee. But mum's the word. Let's just see how he unveils this new project of his. Is there anything else you can tell me that would be useful in conforming this experience to reality?"

"There has been a lot of talk with a theatre up there. I think it's Goodman. Gary has acted as the agent in this and contacted the director, who seems to be an old friend of his. I don't know his name. In any event, you know Tom liked what Gary did with *A Perfect Analysis Given By a Parrot* and *The Frosted Glass Coffin* in Atlanta. Gary has got Tennessee to agree to the production of these two, under his direction at the Goodman, along with a new play he's working on. You'll love the title. It's *Some Problems for the Moose Lodge.*"

I laughed. This was Tennessee in his best form of irony. Submitting the emotional stew of his characters to the members of a Moose Lodge for a solution was a great comic idea. And it really said something about the futility of most human intervention. "If that's a new title and a new play, then there's still hope for him," I said.

"Unfortunately, I don't think Gary's got a sense of humor. It's my impression that his work tends towards pretentiousness. Just the other night, I heard Gary and Schuy trying to get Tom to change the title from *Some Problems for the Moose Lodge* to something dumb and faggoty like *House of Papier Mâché.* The real problem for you, of course, is how much of a role you wish to play in all this. You're going to hate what you see going on with that little menage Gary's put together."

"I thought I would just call and see if you're engaged for dinner tonight?" said Tennessee when he first called me on this Chicago visit. "It's time I filled you in. I want to spend more time with you now, in the early stage of this production. I hope we can get together so I can tell you all about it." There were voices in the background and a loud fanfare of recorded sound.

"What's that noise, Tennessee?"

"Some friends are just entertaining me with the great Bidu Sayou, a friend from the past. Do you know the Villa Lobos *Bachianas Brasileiras Number 5?* It's my music of the moment."

"Do you think they could turn it down a bit so I could hear you better?"

"I called you especially with it on so that they don't know I'm talking to you. Can we meet for dinner?"

"Sure. You know I want to see you." We agreed on a place for dinner only after I assured Tennessee that it was "our kind of place." That meant cool, dark, comfortable. A good place to talk and relax. But there was a new caveat for restaurant selection. "There must be no salt in anything I consume. None whatsoever. My heart is its bad old self and salt is bad for the blood pressure." I knew the chef where we were going and could see to it that he was given a salt-free dinner. I would act on his request, but these forays into good health practices seemed increasingly symbolic when played against the general activity of his life.

I was sitting at the restaurant when suddenly I felt myself in the powerful embrace of our greatest living playwright. In the time which had elapsed since I had seen him, I had spoken often of him to close friends and, most frequently, to my parents. On these occasions, with varying degrees of humor, Tennessee would be referred to with "how's our boy" (by my octogenarian father) or "any news from the world's greatest living playwright" by my septuagenarian mother. These were fond and friendly references for the troubled person we all knew him to be.

Our boy looked good. "You see," he said, "you are all

right. You're just as robust as I felt you were. We're tough cookies, you and I. It will take more than a Broadway flop to get us down. At least for long." I filed away his reference to my health and did not let him know that I was aware he had told the Key West faction that I might no longer be among the living.

We retired to our table and perused the menu. "There must be salt in everything on this menu," he said. "There's sodium in almost everything, Tennessee, but I can see that the chef doesn't add any salt to just about anything you wish to order." It seemed now that salt could be added to the ongoing list of worldly things which were out to get him. I asked that the chef come to the table and explained the exigencies of the situation. Overawed by his patron, the chef made notes and retired to assemble the salt-free, but still aesthetically-pleasing, fare for which he was known.

"I don't know anyone else who can get things done like that," said Tennessee. "Everyone else I know seems lost in restaurants. It's a helpful skill, knowing how to get along in restaurants."

"A restaurant is a hell of a place to get lost in, Tennessee. But let's put that behind us. I'm very anxious to know what you're working on now."

"I've got a book I'm working on with a friend. And there are two plays in addition to the three we'll be producing here at the Goodman Theatre. The book's *The Bag People*. My good friend, who's of Italian descent and very resourceful, has some wonderful photographic prints of the bag women in Manhattan. I've written some text to go around the pictures. Interpretive captions and humorous asides. He's got a publisher so there shouldn't be any problem getting it out soon."

This was information to be filed under the crystal crocodile. I didn't think that a book poking fun at the urban indigent would do much for Tennessee's image and I told him so. It just seemed another exploitive move on some seductive person's part to gain Tennessee's cooperation in a venture which could only harm him.

"Maybe you'll approve of my plays for the Goodman, then," he said. "Two of them were produced by Gary Tucker with a good success in Atlanta. I have persuaded him to attempt to duplicate that success here in Chicago. I have also added a third play to the group, called *Some Problems for the Moose Lodge*. It's actually a work in progress and could become a full-length play. As for now, it's a one-act comedy, though in the mood of the others, which just might be called in the mood of black humor, if that term still has any currency. Gary has impressed me very much. He kindly agreed to stay with me in Key West to begin work on these productions. He very kindly brought his friend Schuyler Wyatt with him. I believe I introduced them to you some time back. Schuy is so talented. He has volunteered to write some music and a song which will serve as a theme for *Moose Lodge*. In fact, I have been so impressed with his talent, that I have contacted Juilliard to see if I might secure a grant or fellowship for him. Then, of course, I would look in on him whenever I was in New York."

I knew that this would come as close as he ever would to revealing the true nature of his devotion to the talented Schuyler Wyatt. I was amused at the baroque embellishments he was using to touch up the true picture. I was upset that he was allowing his personal life to become so involved in the production of his plays. This was in direct contradiction of his policy during his less corrupt period. I remembered that he would have nothing to do with actors or stage people in general, even to the point of turning down all the opportunistic male beauties who came his way through the years. But I didn't really want to spend what time I had with Tennessee talking about Gary and Schuy.

172   BRUCE SMITH

"You seem to have recovered a bit from New York, Tennessee," I said. "Those openings are not good for the health."

"I ultimately took some of the advice I gave to Edward Albee just after his *Who's Afraid of Virginia Woolfe* opened on Broadway. I told him he would be wise to engage in activities outside of his own work. In that way he would keep safe from the block that arises from the self-consciousness which Broadway imposes on an honest playwright who it considers dangerously so. So I've been busy painting. There's a new portrait of Schuyler that will be one of my best works in that medium once I've finished with it."

So that's what he was doing with Schuyler in Key West. Painting. "But you mentioned two new plays, Tennessee. What are they?"

"What I am looking for is always the same thing. One play grows out of another play and it is obviously related to it with very few exceptions. But even if I don't find the exact thing I'm looking for, I think that I find each time some new trace of it, some clue. It may be embarrassing to say that I am looking for the meaning of human existence, but I can redeem the pomposity of that statement by saying that that's what we are all looking for if we're looking for anything more than the content of our daily lives, something beyond a continuity of days and nights. When Prometheus stole that fire from Mount Olympus, he provided us with an image that would distinguish man and beast. A beast doesn't look for meanings, baby—at least I don't believe so—but when Prometheus stole that fire he gave us a symbol for something we humans have stolen, an equally dangerous thing, the romantic search for meaning. The search is going on, and the object of the search has not been very completely discovered.

"My new plays are, then, an extension of my search, though I am trying to make my work seem more contemporary. I believe I told you before about *Masks Outrageous and Obscure.* About the wealthiest woman in the world and her quest for meaning beyond the power of her wealth. She's based on a Hungarian woman I've never met, but who's corresponded with me occasionally. She sends me fascinating letters after she's seen the Budapest production of my plays. She's evidently immensely wealthy, if such there may be in even an enlightened Communist regime. But she has a deep understanding of my plays and their meaning for life. She once wrote, 'Thank you for *A Streetcar Named Desire.* I perceived its every line, every mystery of motive, deep in my soul. Who may you be? What kind of physician, engineer, or maybe sorcerer, before whose searching glance there are no secrets? This is some divine gift which makes you able to see what is possible to happen. You open crystal heights and disclose the depths. And you always find the solution for the human and give back my hope again!' Her name is Eva Laszlo and she is unforgettable although we've never met. But you see, baby, I will find her in my play. Her and perhaps a few more traces of the meaning of human existence."

"This is exciting, Tennessee. Then this woman, this richest woman in the world, is a kind of Blanche du Bois who is now empowered with wealth and position?"

"Yes, I think so. Blanche is still alive to me. She said all she could at the time of *Streetcar.* But she was disenfranchised and powerless to continue her search, although she did find some meaning in the kindness she depended upon in strangers. This new play will be on a world stage. I want Vanessa Redgrave to play the lead."

"Shouldn't we tell the world about this, Tennessee? This is the best news the theatre world has had in decades. Let's let the press know about this right away."

"I thought I might just spark your interest with this project. The others will seem small scale to you, but they're what I can handle just now, as long as I have the big play to work on. *Moose Lodge* is painted in broad strokes and in it I have tried to become more consciously contemporary. The new wave of playwrights, at their worst, make a cynical joke of the search for the meaning of life. At their best, they create something which is true, such as the Albee, Pinter, Beckett concept of human existence as an almost indecipherable, ambiguous attempt to reconcile the twin faces of the heart: belief and mockery of that belief. Theirs is great work. A real contribution to the search.

"I don't know how serious some of the even younger generation are in their playwrighting. Take your own Chicago David Mamet for example. He has a true gift of dialogue. People really do talk like that. But to what end? I think his plays are interesting studies in sociology. I was amused, by the way, that in the Chicago program for *Clothes for a Summer Hotel,* instead of profiling the current author, namely myself, they chose to provide several pages of information on Mamet instead. A rather curious occurrence, I thought."

"Be careful what you say about Mamet in this town, Tennessee. If you criticize him, you can be accused of everything from sour grapes to anti-Semitism. He has a real hold here."

"I'll take that under advisement. As for telling the world about *Masks Outrageous and Obscure,* just do as you think best. But don't you think they'll wonder what's going on? Especially after the inauspicious reception for my last major effort, I mean?"

"It's just what the doctor ordered. A great new play in the *Streetcar* tradition, that will star Vanessa Redgrave."

"That should make them sit up and take notice. Maybe even keep them from counting my empty wine bottles."

With that we toasted what promised to be an eventful era for Chicago theatre.

CHAPTER XV

A Geopolitical Countdown

AT EXACTLY 7:32 A.M. of the next day, the phone rang in the top-floor office of my home.

"Don't ever mention Vanessa again," said the unfamiliar voice. "Do you want to bring the entire Goodman board on my head? I've had six calls within the last hour. Did you have to tell the press about his new play? Don't you know about Vanessa's pro-Palestinian politics? You're going to cost me my job. Then where will Tennessee be with his little plays?"

I gathered from the gist of the talk that my morning caller was Greg Mosher, director of the Goodman Theatre. In that I had a healthy respect for his theatre work in Chicago despite almost insurmountable obstacles, I listened with more than the usual sympathy to his litany of woes.

"I'm truly sorry if I've made your work more difficult, Greg, but I'm sure you'll agree that the *Masks Outrageous and Obscure* item was surely newsworthy. And I found it exciting that Tennessee held an actress other than Geraldine Page in such high regard that he could cast her in a play that has the potential of being a *Streetcar* for the modern-day theatre. Don't you agree that that's an exciting possibility? Unlike other factions in this town, I'm capable of separating talent from politics. I agree with Tennessee that Vanessa Redgrave is one of the most accomplished actresses we have. Her combination of enlightened intelligence and physical beauty makes her presence on the stage or films unique. My considerations are always for Tennessee; and any good shot I can give him, I will. It's my impression that his contributions to the theatre will outlast most of what's currently going on the stage here."

"I know you care about Tennessee's welfare," said Mosher. "But I want you to believe that I do as well. No other theatre in the country would undertake a production of his work just now."

"While we're all grateful, Greg, these are productions for the studio theatre. It's not as though you've committed the main stage for the plays. But that's just as well, since you've bought the Tucker act and let him direct."

"That was Tennessee's ultimatum. I had to buy Gary and Schuyler Wyatt if he was to lend his name to the productions as well as the new play, *Some Problems for the Moose Lodge*. It's not what I would have done, but believe me, we're giving Tennessee the full resources of the theatre. It's a great opportunity for him to work creatively with a sympathetic staff."

"I know you're fighting the good fight, Greg. Forgive me if I say that I find it unbelievable that people can be roused to such passion by the mere mention of an actress. Even if the idea goes through, the production is a good two years away and I doubt very much that Goodman will have anything to do with it. Don't you agree?"

"Just try not to mention her again. I've got enough to do to keep this operation functional without troubleshooting brushfires like this."

"You have my word. I won't talk to the press about Vanessa again. At least until this production has run its course."

This was as good a way as any to begin the day's reflections on what was really going on with our boy now that he was back in town. Though he had seemed to be operating in the rational mode that had brought me together with him in the first place, I could sense that he was at a critical point in his professional spiral. In making plans for his important new play he was imaginatively extending his career upward. But the daily reality was that he was corrupting his own values by bringing lovers and hangers-on into the important work of his plays. It was difficult to discern just how conscious he was of the profound deterioration of his work ethic. And the Machiavellian work of Gary Tucker in tackling Tennessee at his weakest—and most weakening—points, sex and drugs, was succeeding beyond even Tucker's wildest fantasies.

This grim vision was interrupted by another, still early-morning call. This time it was a recognizable voice. It was Aaron Gold, show business columnist for the *Chicago Tribune*.

"Well, you've managed to get everyone's attention with this morning's item about Vanessa Redgrave. You'd better just tell your friend to be a little more careful about his casting. He's just about used up our tolerance, in case you didn't know that. You're not really a show business person, anyway, so I don't know what you're doing with Tennessee."

"I believe it's one of Tennessee's brighter moves of recent years. That is, to have a friend who has nothing to lose in show business terms. He needs that kind of objectivity, and that's what I intend to provide for him." Gold had been after me ever since owner Nancy Goldberg excluded him from the head table at a luncheon for Princess Margaret at Maxim's de Paris. He was at the next best table, but that evidently wasn't good enough. I had never heard the end of it.

Promptly at nine, I called Tennessee.

"The fat's in the fire this time, baby," he chortled. "Maybe we'd better just keep our plans to ourselves until we're in a better position to defend them. I rather gather that I'm here under a kind of special moral dispensation which we must not violate. I've already talked with Kup today and I promised we'd keep as quiet as possible. So, no more items for a while, baby."

"Tennessee, if things went wrong with *Clothes*, the conditions under which you're operating here on the new production look even less likely to succeed. They've made you accept a studio production, which I think is demeaning to your stature. And you've made your own contribution to the cause by hiring Tucker as your director. His reputation as a director of gay, campy farces can't do much to enhance this new work."

"I know you haven't taken to Gary Tucker, but he did some most creditable work on two short plays of mine in Atlanta. And, of course, Schuyler Wyatt's contributions to the music for *Moose Lodge* is quite a remarkable achievement, in my opinion. In any event, I was calling to invite you to lunch today and to dinner tonight, if you're free to join us."

"Us?"

"In the interests of economy, I have come to share a suite here at the Delaware Towers with Gary and Schuy. We take some of our meals here. Could you stop by at noon? You can see my situation here in Chicago and we can go on for lunch wherever you please."

Curiosity about the new menage was too great to deny. "He's always late, you know." I could hear Tennessee's voice as I was about to rap on the door to his suite. It was five minutes past the hour. "That must be him now. Be good."

For the summer season, Tennessee affected an exaggerated Panama hat. With his dark glasses and white suit he looked like the quintessential Caribbean con man.

Gary and Schuy were dressed to go. "Tennessee just wants a hamburger for lunch, so don't try to take us to any place fancy," Gary Tucker said. "And I'm on a diet, so I want a salad or some seafood," said Schuyler Wyatt.

The operative word was obviously budget, so I steered them to the local Hamburger Hamlet.

Settled into our lunch, Tucker observed, "We've got to be careful with the press. The Goodman thing is something that has to be handled carefully. Aaron and Kup want to know what's going on. I can handle Aaron. I've known him since *Turds in Hell* and *Whores of Babylon*." He uttered the titles of these two productions as though they were *Hedda Gabbler* and *Miss Julie*. "Aaron will do anything I say, but Kup's another matter."

"Frankly, Gary, I'm more concerned about what Richard Christiansen (the *Tribune*'s drama critic) and Glenna Syse (the same role at the *Sun Times*) are going to say. They're the ones who will make or break this production."

"I don't know them. But you've got to be careful with Aaron. He doesn't like it that you're associated with Tennessee. After all, his major claim to fame before he became the *Tribune*'s key columnist was a relationship with Zsa Zsa Gabor which culminated with a 2:00 A.M. rendezvous at Franksville for some hot dogs."

"With friends like you, Mr. Tucker, I'm certain Mr. Gold needs no additional enemies. Shall we move along to

some perhaps airier topic of conversation?" said Tennessee.
He obviously had some conscious clue to Tucker's character.
That was reassuring.

"How's the casting, Tennessee? Are you pleased with the
local crop of talent?" I asked.

"Only time will tell, baby. But there's a rehearsal this
afternoon. Why don't you join us at the theatre and see for
yourself?"

Tucker jumped in: "Tennessee, we can't have Bruce over
there this early on. Let's wait until we have something more
finished for him to see? You know the cast doesn't like
strangers in the audience at this stage."

Clearly, Tucker was afraid I would tip their hand to the
press at every opportunity. I had no such ambition. I could
wait to see these plays.

"Now, Gary," Tennessee said, "we can't just hide our
lamp under a bushel with Bruce. I know there are some
difficulties in this relationship with you, but he is my
friend and I think I still have the authority to invite whom I
please to a rehearsal of three of my plays."

"Thank you, Tennessee. I do appreciate your invitation.
I want to see these plays very much. But I can wait a few
days until Gary has his act more together."

"Dinner's at eight tonight at the suite," said Tennessee.
"Gary Tucker's cooking so you're on your own in that
department. I'm going to swim now and then go over to
the Goodman. I will want you to join me over there one day
soon, despite the evident opposition."

CHAPTER XVI

Bidu Sayou and the
Etiquette of Control

THERE WAS A PARTY going on in Tennessee's suite at the Delaware Towers. I could hear it all the way from the elevator at the end of the hall. The wild dithyramb of Bidu Sayou's renowned rendition of the Villa Lobos' *Bachianas Brasileiras Number 5* careened through the thin hotel doors.

Gary opened the door in an apron. There was the aroma of good Southern Italian food in the air. The Pullman kitchen doors had been pulled back and Gary was addressing himself to the meal's preparation.

Among the assembled guests were some of the troupe from the Chicago Opera board whom I had seen at a distance before. And, ensconced beside Tennessee, the newly-minted composer, Schuyler Wyatt. "Hello, baby," Tennessee called exuberantly. "There's some red wine around here somewhere. These boys don't seem to know too much about it. Their 'drug of choice,' I believe the term is, is something other." The something other betrayed its presence with its pungent smoke.

The sound of the Villa Lobos was so loud and so irritating in its tinniness as played back through the cheap tape recorder that it was impossible to carry on a conversation. It became apparent that this was another of Gary's theatrical ploys to keep Tennessee and I from speaking to one another. But in this I was determined.

Crouched in the position of a Turkish courtier beside Tennessee and Schuy was one of the opera people. He was presumably wildly stoned, because he just continued to gaze open-mouthed with rapture at the two of them on the couch. Tennessee lurched forward and looked into his face. "Nice teeth," he said and began to laugh as he settled back down with Schuy.

The Villa Lobos had blissfully ceased its assault on the room. I sat down next to Tennessee.

"How do you find the Goodman studio, Tennessee? The stage is so restricted that I've only seen chamber dramas performed on it with any kind of success. Will it do for you?"

Tennessee opened his mouth to speak. Instantly, Bidu Sayou screeched into the room again. There was Gary, adjusting the volume upwards with one hand while turning over the Italian sausage with the other. I thought instantly that this was some kind of trailer park psychodrama, where the sound of domestic squalor is drowned out with the electronic cooperation of Tammy Wynette.

Tennessee's attention span under the influence of the wine and the grass was limited. As soon as the Villa Lobos began to play, he turned his attention from me back to Schuy and Nice Teeth.

This wasn't my kind of party and Gary was making that abundantly clear. There would be no transmission of information to me about the Goodman productions. How pleased the absent Aaron Gold must be by this, I surmised.

Since the prevailing scale of manners at this function was that of a barnyard, I decided to take matters in hand. I rose and turned off the tape recorder. The silence sliced through the group like a knife. The room froze as if the recorder had been their lifeline. "I just want to talk to Tennessee for a few minutes without having to scream at him. Then I'll go in peace and you can go on with your party."

"Hmmm," said Tennessee. "Let's just go into the other room to talk for awhile. We can then allow the other guests to enjoy themselves."

"My number's up, you know," he said as soon as we were in the next room. "I'm too old and too tired to fight anymore. I can just hope that some luck will come my way to see me through these last plays. I know you want to help me, have helped me, but what can you do now? You can't direct plays, can you?"

He was being both facetious and not.

"I have no theatrical ambitions, as you know, Tennessee. But there are other, better directors than Gary Tucker in Chicago. I don't think we'll have enough personal time together for me to go into this at length, but I can safely predict that this new production won't work out with any success. You have even less of a chance now than you did with *Clothes* in New York. Now, you're mixing drugs with alcohol and sex with your job. I hate what Gary has done to you. He's trapped you. He knows I'm fool enough to try to get you out, but he's not going to make that attempt easy. And it seems that you're going along for the ride with no protest."

"I know you read these situations clearly, Bruce. But we can't talk here. The boys have to have their party, you know. Can you come to the theatre tomorrow afternoon?

Then we can break and have a nice long talk about it at dinner tomorrow night. I can't say more now. I just can't."

"We probably won't have another chance to make these plans, so when and where shall I meet you?"

"Just come on over to the studio about two o'clock. Now, we really mustn't keep my guests waiting any longer."

The next afternoon at the theatre Tennessee would reassure me that he was practicing his old mode of daily writing in the early morning and then having a swim. That he had been struck a body blow by the New York critics; that he doubted he would ever recover from it; and that Gary and Schuy were offering him solace.

"The more you depart from the strong, assertive personality you presented to me when we first met, the less I know what my role becomes for you. But I feel a kind of special mission for you, Tennessee. You know I'll help you all I can, and that against all advice from my Chicago friends."

"We have something, don't we? I can't imagine coming back to Chicago and not seeing you. But you know that's not going to be easy with my current cast. They see you as a threat, not to me, but to them. You're a touchstone for me. Let's try to remember that we're important to each other and that we appreciate each other. We'll have dinner without them tonight and we can talk more then."

Gary then arrived, with Schuy carrying his now signature guitar case. He would be Orpheus, but the descent would be Tennessee's.

CHAPTER XVII

When Wine Redeems
the Sight

IF WE WERE TO take Strindberg, another playwright with women much on his mind, as an example, then an essential ingredient for all creative work is chaos. Tennessee had said that he found his writing so intense that regular life paled in comparison. To make life endurable, he had to balance out the intensity and make his regular life more equal to the writing. Throughout his life that would seem to have been the pattern. In trying to rationalize the present *mise en scene* of Tennessee's life, I thought hopefully that, if nothing else, the present state of affairs might contribute to his work.

In a sense, I was correct in this. But there was a new twist to the alchemy of his art. As his last play emerged, it seemed the transmutation of almost daily events went immediately into the staged action and dialog.

It was in this thoughtful state of mind that I next saw Tennessee, before he returned to Key West after having completed the first stage of Goodman negotiations for the fall production of A *Perfect Analysis Given by a Parrot*, *The Frosted Glass Coffin*, and *Some Problems for the Moose Lodge*.

We met for dinner at a little bistro called Bastille, which a friend had ingeniously created from his fond memories of Paris trips. It was the kind of place Tennessee and I both liked. Informal, easy, with fairly straightforward food.

"I feel I owe you some kind of explanation of things, beginning with what went on in New York with *Clothes* and now with the present situation both in Key West and the Delaware Towers.

"You're worried about me, I can always tell that. But let me try to explain. I'm going to check out soon. This is probably my last go around. I'm more aware of the present limitations than you might think. I'm tired now, Bruce. There isn't the time for all the different aspects of life which I once chose to live. It's just more efficient for me to live like this right now.

"You've made it clear that you don't like what you call the faggot arrangements I've made. I know you think they're faggot arrangements, but they're all I can handle right now. Gary's done some good work for me before this, on *Perfect Analysis* and *Glass Coffin*. You know these later plays of mine have received a not very sympathetic audience and very little sympathetic production. I think he showed some enterprise, you know, in doing those productions in Atlanta. And, more mysteriously, he's found me Schuyler Wyatt. I've had to resort to hustlers of late. Surely you think this arrangement is at least safer for me."

"I can understand what you're saying, Tennessee, but let me offer you my own perspective. For better or worse, I always interpret a professional person's activities in the light of the media. Since the media is so important to you, and has been ever since Claudia Cassidy and Ashton Ste-

vens gave *Menagerie* their support and, really, started you
on your career. People in Chicago only know Gary as the
director of two camp plays, *Whores of Babylon* and *Turds in
Hell*. Why lend instant support to the critics' preconceived
notions that your late plays are inferior by letting a director
handle them who has only those highly specious credentials?"

"You probably don't understand camp, baby. There's
nothing wrong with a little judicious application of camp
in the theatre, you know. Gary has convinced me of that.
He seems to feel that I should loosen up a little and 'get
with it,' I believe the expression is. There has always been
plenty of humor in my plays, dark though it may be. Gary
has convinced me that this new age of theatre demands
more humor."

"But your humor has always been cast as irony, which is
an acceptable manner for handling humor in the context of
a tragedy. Are you planning to make a laughing matter out
of the psychic trauma familiar to most of your characters?
When Jim told me you were working on a play called *Some
Problems for the Moose Lodge* I thought you were on to a
perfect resolution of your search for a way to dramatize the
irony of tragedy, if we may use that expression. It's a
wonderful title and helpful to the audience in beginning to
explain what your new direction might be. Before this,
they've just been put off by a seeming slapstick approach to
tragedy which a superficial reading might imply."

"I liked that title, too. But we may have to do without it
if Gary and Schuy have their way. They want to call it *House
of Papier Mâché*. It's rather obvious, don't you think? But
they think the audience will understand it better that way."

"I'm sorry, Tennessee, but any advantage you may now
see in your arrangements with this duo is completely un-
dermined by what they're doing to your creative work and

thereby to your reputation. No one would care or even be very much surprised if you were seen making violent love to Schuy in the middle of the Michigan Avenue bridge. Your reputation as a writer would survive it. But what your reputation won't survive is the kind of silliness you're describing to me now. Letting them retitle your plays and direct them in the manner of fag-camp. It's obvious that they want to drag you down to their own level. You certainly can't raise them to your own."

"When I'm with them, it seems an easy matter to make these concessions."

"How much of it is done under the influence of pot or booze, Tennessee? Try to look at this clearly and see how important it is that you keep your perspective. I think that Greg and the Goodman are trying to give you a good shot, even if it is only a studio production. Greg seems to have indicated that the new play is a work in progress and might go onto the main stage ultimately. Do you really have to parade all this nonsense before the public? Do you really want to see your byline in print beside a title like *House of Papier Mâché?*"

"You've made your point," he said, rather angrily. "You remind me of Elia Kazan sometimes. At the time of the production of *Sweet Bird of Youth,* I had a real go around with him about the way he interpreted the third act of that play. I accused him of identifying me with the Princess and in saying so meaning that he thought I was actually a cheap, pretentious old bitch. A poseur, not capable of real passion for anything but the next drink. I admitted at the time that he might be right, but only in a limited way. Even then I was haunted by the idea of my own death as an artist. And I am always haunted by that terror. It's why I drink as I do and why I keep on working. While I'm still working I can still justify my existence and shout out 'It just ain't so!' "

"If that's the way you feel, why provide ammunition to the press and to your audiences to the contrary? You're certainly through if you're abrogating your work to the ministrations of ambitious persons using, it would seem, sexual and emotional blackmail to control you."

"I've had about enough lessons from you just now, young man," he growled. I thought he would get up and leave. But he finished off a glass of red wine and held the empty glass expectantly up to the waiter, who had rushed over at the sound of raised voices.

"Let's switch to another subject, shall we," I suggested. "Perhaps you could tell me what happened to you and *Clothes* once I left New York."

"I don't have to tell you it was a nightmare of the worst proportions. And the day after the opening I didn't know where you'd gone. Maria just said you didn't want to have any more to do with me and just took off for destinations unknown. I tried to save the play by financing an additional one-week run, which was as ill advised as your telegram suggested it might be. I then fled to Key West, Maria in tow who tried to calm my ravaged nerves. Gary and Schuy were there and became more obliging in their efforts to sustain me. Maria finally left after I assured her she was still in the will." At this, he laughed.

"Did you ever have a postmortem with Geraldine Page, to try and determine the motivation for her strange behavior throughout the run?"

"She was dead set against doing another play with Rip. They had recently done *Hamlet* together, you know. She refused to speak to me, except to suggest that I should make a concerted effort to put more of my talent into my work than creating havoc with people's lives. I'm sure you would agree with her there." He chuckled again.

"If I could see that you thrived on the chaos or that your work did, perhaps I could understand it better. But it all seems so self-defeating at this point. Speaking of which, how's your brother these days?"

"To my understanding, he's taking care of mother. Miss Edwina is now confined to a nursing home. Dakin sends on photographs which do nothing but depress me. She looks mummified or, more accurately, recently exhumed. It can't be long now. He thinks I should come on down to visit her, but why visit a mummy? I should think they could take but little pleasure in it, you know. Dakin is just across the river by expressway. His only redeeming feature, aside from his hilarious eccentricities, is his continued attention to mother."

"And what will you do now, before rehearsals begin at Goodman this fall?"

"I'll return to Key West with Gary and Schuy. There I'll continue to work on *Moose Lodge* and try to finish my portrait of Schuy."

"Do you paint only men, Tennessee?"

"An interesting question, considering my plays are mostly women oriented, which I gather was your point. I did paint one woman. Marian Vaccaro. She was my great friend, perished now from drink. Those who have seen it think it a good likeness. She was a kind and sensitive soul. She once said to me about death, 'We all die, of course, but sometimes it may be a bit gentler to have a dream to dream.' "

CHAPTER XVIII

Laughter of the Dark

CHICAGO HAD TURNED COLD by the time of Tennessee's return. It was November and an early snow blew diagonally against the black banners which snapped from the street lamps around the Goodman Theatre. On them emblazoned: "Tennessee Laughs."

Tennessee and I stood side by side, looking through the snow at these strange banners. I imagined another banner crossing with them, that new pennant of some pain, the bottle of Seconal crossed with the crystal crocodile. Only with that banner waving did the message of the other make sense.

As we waited for the light, the banners furled and unfurled. "Are they talking about the same Tennessee Williams, do you suppose," I asked.

"Baby, I just don't have much choice just now. I've been told by the best authority I know that I'm lucky to be tolerated here. We just have to go along with the gag, if such it is meant to be."

"I'm afraid the laugh's on you, Tennessee. The Goodman board has obviously forced Greg's hand and demanded that he make this project as marketable as possible. I guess they think if they say 'Tennessee Laughs,' your work can be sold as a couple of glib hours in the manner of Neil Simon. Does that please you much?"

"Gary says it isn't that bad. He says the plays really are funny. He's going to play them for humor. But why not wait a few more minutes? You'll see for yourself during the rehearsals."

As we settled into the uncomfortable Goodman Studio seats, I said: "I have to say, Tennessee—and I have to say it quickly before Greg and Gary come in—that, in comparison to what you're subscribing to here at the Goodman, your stature in New York for *Clothes* was at least heroic. By going along with this banal merchandising program, you're asking for all you're inevitably going to get. I just don't see how this can work out well for you."

It rapidly became apparent that the three plays which composed the program called "Tennessee Laughs" were no laughing matter. In addition to the two plays which Tucker had directed before in Atlanta (*A Perfect Analysis Given by a Parrot* and *The Frosted Glass Coffin*), the theatre was offering up the work in progress, *Some Problems for the Moose Lodge*. Though this last work would seem to have benefited in levity from viewings of "The Carol Burnett Show," it was still a very dark work indeed, dealing as it did with premature death by alcoholism, senility, mendacity, and insanity. And though Tennessee and Gary chuckled, guffawed, and even laughed uproariously during these rehearsals, neither Greg nor I had the stomach for it. As humor, Tucker's direction was superficial and slapstick. I could see that the actors were suffering.

"Perhaps this is something new for you, Tennessee.

With 'Tennessee Laughs' you're putting both the actors and the audience in a false position from the start."

"If your critique weren't so patently overshadowed by your clear dislike for Mr. Tucker I might give some credence to it," Tennessee snarled. "But as it is I gather I cannot rely upon you for a clear and honest opinion of this work. Perhaps we should discontinue our association for the duration of this production."

"Tennessee, I can only say okay with pleasure since I'm getting nothing but pain from this mess you're in. But let me say one last thing. I know you have a sense of humor, and I know as well as anyone how you distribute an ironic touch through the tragedy of your best plays. But you are not and never have been a humorist in the theatre. By going along with this pathetic gag called 'Tennessee Laughs' you're indulging in a monumental act of self-betrayal. The critics won't know whether you've lost your mind entirely or if this farce is being forced from you at gunpoint. It is something like gunpoint, isn't it, Tennessee?"

"You still hold out some sad hope for my sanity, do you? Then let me work. My writing is all I have that saves my sanity."

"So we've been told, time out of mind. Those of us who still love you want you to work, but for yourself, not for scatty opportunists who seem to have captured your passing fancy. You're playing this one very close to the bone, Tennessee, and you're making it next to impossible for those who want to help you to do so with any effectiveness. We can no longer resort to the comfort of the notion that chaos is good for your work. I'm sorry to seem unkind, but none of what's going on right now is very good. If we're left without the artistic benefit of chaos in your life, then you must try to forgive us for ceasing to wish to tolerate it."

"I sure guess you're not a theatre person, to have said all

that. If I were the vengeful sort I could see that you never
worked in the theatre again." He was quite darkly angry. But
still, he kept standing there in the lobby of the Goodman,
hesitating from making some kind of memorable exit.

"I've never believed you were that kind of person, Tennessee, and I still don't. It's just that all this is so tacky. Have
you somehow shut off your radar, to be unaware of that?"

"I told you before that I'm only just tolerated here.
That's more than I am anywhere else at the moment. I seem
to have some magical belief that Chicago will continue to
bring me luck. It has so often in the past that I'm willing
to indulge this present project with the slight hope that it
may succeed in some way. What else would you suggest,
since you seem to have given this matter some prior
thought?" He had a slight smile now and his right eye
glinted up at me.

"The first thing I'd do is use whatever legal power you
have to strike those goddamned 'Tennessee Laughs' banners. Then produce the three plays as they were presumably
written, with a new director. Let Greg direct them. He's
intelligent and knows your work."

"It's all too late now, baby. The die is cast. I can only
hope you're wrong. By the way, I have to cancel our dinner
engagement tonight. Not because of this conversation,
baby, please believe that. It would seem that you are not
alone in your concern about the direction of these plays.
One of your critics has summoned me to a dinner confer-
ence. I am full of apprehension. Gary doesn't want me to
go, but I feel I must do whatever I can to work smoothly
with the press. I've been a reluctant student in this, but
you've had something to do with teaching me its wisdom."
He laughed, rather darkly. But he gave me his coyote hug
and I was glad that I had spoken my mind.

Tennessee called promptly at 9:00 A.M. the next morning.
"I'll say one thing, baby, about those banners you like so much.

They've made certain persons sit up and take notice. I guess I have to take what you said yesterday under advisement, in the light of the conversation I had last night at dinner with Glenna Syse, the drama critic for the *Chicago Sun-Times*."

"Glenna's the critic who gave you the good review for *Clothes, Tennessee*. I hope you had a good meeting with her. She's one of our best writers."

"I wish you had been able to join us. We just sat and talked amiably enough for awhile. Enough of a while for me to wonder what it was all about. But after the second martini on the rocks, the lady revealed she was a pistol-packin' mama. She said she wouldn't tolerate a play that made fun of old people. She then went on to say that she had a mother in a nursing home and that it was not funny. She threatened to blackball the plays if I said anything humorous about sick old people. Seems you people here in Chicago are keeping a pretty close eye on me, to all appearances. What do you think about this new development? Should I flee the city before opening night?"

"I think that Glenna was referring more to the inappropriateness of a humorous approach to situations which cause people extreme pain, Tennessee. In this instance it isn't really seen as therapeutic to laugh, but rather as insensitive. I told you to strike those banners, Tennessee. How is the cast reacting to Gary's direction of your material as farce?"

"It's slow going. I don't know if we've got the actress for Bella in *Moose Lodge*. Why not come on down to the theatre later this afternoon. Then we can go from there to an early dinner somewhere."

"I'm surprised to be asked."

"I know your heart's in the right place, baby. Just don't say anything to Greg and Gary. Let me do the talking."

The small confines and the poor lighting of the Goodman Studio lent the proceedings a kind of claustrophobic, Beckett-like aura. However, the experience was revelatory.

Facing the stage were such veteran actors as the fine Les Podewell, who had among other career achievements travelled with the Russian Art Theatre in the 30's. The appreciation for working with new material from Tennessee Williams was palpable among the entire cast, but most so among its veteran performers. When they would see him at rehearsals, their energy level soared and the play's language really began to sing. But there was an aura of heartbreak on the stage as well as they saw the playwright shroud himself in the directorial technique of Gary Tucker. For me, their plea was obvious. Let us do our best with this less-than-great Tennessee Williams and that means getting some less heavy-handed direction. Photographs from the period always show a delighted, even giggly, cast whenever Tennessee was among them. The defeat of their enchantment came from the hired hand.

Some Problems for the Moose Lodge proved more a diary in dialog form than a true play. Its themes were those which concerned Tennessee personally at the time he was writing: obesity, alcoholism, premature death, insanity, the futility of contemporary existence. Conversation heard one day would appear in the play's new dialog the next. Intriguingly, Tennessee once again focused his frustrations about the progress of the play on the female lead. Marji Banks played Bella, the mother, who was supposed to be two hundred pounds overweight. By nature a slim woman, Banks's rendering into fat was a daily cosmic chore.

"Aren't obese persons heavy by definition?" Tennessee asked one day at rehearsals. "The padding confines her movement so that she looks like a miniaturized float in a Macy's parade." It was true.

"These people are valiantly trying to survive in the further reaches of dragon country," he growled. "We can't have them floating about the stage like Mardi Gras balloons."

"Are there no fat actresses available in the Midwest?" he

inquired. "Couldn't we lend the proceedings a hand by being as lifelike as possible?"

Everyone felt sorry for Marji Banks for not being fat. And being aware that she was under fire did not produce her best work.

When Tennessee presented himself at rehearsals, the cast came alive with suggestions of their own for the advancement of the plays. Tennessee always listened with great sympathy and humorous attention to their individual interpretations of their roles in the three plays. There would be inspired moments when the action and character of the plays seemed to hold together. Then, once the author's presence was removed, the director effectively erased any trace of that inspiration in order to advance his own vision of the production.

On the way from the theatre, Tennessee commented, "I've found in the past that actors often have notions of value to the performance of my plays. Sadly, the only time these personal insights seem to be given much play is when the entire production is suffering from a weakness of direction, if you know what I mean."

"Are you going to let these actors carry the day, then, Tennessee?"

"Gary is just finding his feet in the theatre. We must give him time. In any event, none of these actors has the stature to make meaningful direction to any of the plays. But I like the group very much. Your good, basic, healthy, robust Midwest type." He laughed warmly.

At dinner, he talked about the films that had been made from his plays. "The Hays office effectively castrated *Cat* as I've said before. *Streetcar* is a great film, if I may say so, even if the ending was rendered a bit differently by Kazan than I had originally written it. But the film has integrity and to have Vivien retrieved for other generations is a great accomplishment."

"The first film of yours that I saw was *The Fugitive Kind* at Graumann's Chinese Theatre on Hollywood Boulevard."

"The setting could not be more appropriate, could it? All those street people, those gypsies on the Hollywood strip, they are the fugitive kind. The critics agree with me that it was one of the most successful transfers of a playscript to screenplay of my work. Brando and Magnani were magnificent."

"Did Brando make much of a contribution to the direction of the film?"

"Brando always did his own thing, had his own inner vision. But Anna Magnani had her hand in right from the start. She was passionate about the original play, *Orpheus Descending,* and insisted from pre-production days that she have approval of all changes in sequence and dialog from the original play. Ordinarily, this kind of star performance is not taken affirmatively, but she was a great lady and a dear friend. Her insights gave me a passport to some control over the film, you know. When she said, 'These are characters who become familiar with sadness, before they reach despair. They become hysterical only when the drama forces them to it,' she had won my attention. However, it should not be overlooked that whenever it came time for a little emendation of the script, it was always her most urgent contention that Val's role be reduced in some way. Brando did not react kindly to this, as you can imagine." He chuckled and looked up to me, sipping his red wine.

"Well," I said, "we could wish for Magnani now as Bella. Perhaps she could whip *Moose Lodge* et al. into shape."

"We won't tell Gary this, but Magnani would have taken one look, grabbed him by the nape of the neck, and pushed him out the door, all the while insisting it was for his own good." He laughed.

True perhaps. But then what would she have made of the play itself?

CHAPTER XIX

Lap Robes of Sable, Barrels of Roederer Cristal

"THERE ARE OTHER EXAMPLES of tragic humorists, you know baby," Tennessee said one day toward the opening of the lugubrious trio misleadingly entitled *Tennessee Laughs*. "Think of Mozart and his *Don Giovanni*. Wouldn't that qualify?"

"It is probably the example of that genre of art, Tennessee, but it is also probably Mozart's greatest work. You yourself have admitted that the plays in *Dragon Country* were written quickly and do not rank with *Streetcar* or *Cat*."

"I don't think speed has anything to do with the quality of art. Mozart was notorious for writing scores at white-hot speed without need for a single erasure."

Here Tennessee touched on an area that came to concern him greatly in his last three years. As his physical and psychic energy diminished, his writing weakened as well, which he knew. This was his most painful subject. What was creativity? What was its source? In his darkest moments, he seemed to consider that his genius was independent of himself, that he was just a conduit of some kind, just the mechanical scribe of material that emanated from a source beyond himself. He would come to talk of God more often in our last times together. His last letter, written a few months before he died, concluded with his last written determination of his own personal belief.

We lunched alone the day of the opening. He was in a humorous and even discursive mood, having learned that this production would lead to the production of *Moose Lodge* as a full-length play in the spring of the next year. Greg Mosher had kindly given him this to hang onto, and it considerably reduced the end-of-the-world anxiety which normally attended Tennessee's openings.

"Schuy wants to retitle *Moose Lodge,* you know. He and Gary don't think anyone will understand the humor in it and that, if they do, it will only alienate the conservative Midwest audience. They're so heavily involved that I feel I should give some attention to their insights."

"Surely not *House of Papier Mâché?* It sounds like a project in a grade school crafts class."

"Schuy and Gary think it hints at the insubstantiality of existence and, presumably, of values."

"But the *Moose Lodge* title indicates a meaning of a more subtle nature. If you were known for nothing else, you would certainly be remembered for your titles."

"Those titles don't always come immediately to mind, baby. You know that *Streetcar* was first called *Poker Night?*"

"Well, this time I think you hit onto the right title right off."

"We have some time to think about it, in any event. Something rather touching, rather sad occurred the other day at our suite at the Delaware Towers. Schuy had a gift for me and, as such have not been offered with any frequency, I was moved. But, upon reflection, I was rather horrified. The note read, 'Some good poetry that is also popular.' I guess these two guys of another generation are trying to get me to get with it. The gift, unfortunately, was the recording of *Jonathan Livingston Seagull*. I have forbidden the expenditure for a phonograph to play it, so I'm safe enough 'til we get back to Key West."

"You'll fly back to Key West right after the opening tonight?"

"Unless you have another suggestion. I did offer you a trip to Key West. You have yet to accept."

"I can't just now. It's a busy time of the year for me. Will you go to Sicily soon? It seems a destination of spiritual renewal for you."

"Perhaps, but I have one great curiosity insofar as travel is concerned. According to my agents, I have now accumulated something very much like $6 million in royalties for my plays in the Soviet Union. I'm terrified by their moral puritanism and the efficiency of their secret police, second to none in the world, according to reliable sources. I can't take the money out. If I were to have any benefit from it, I would have to spend it as rubles in Russia itself."

"They're just holding the money in an escrow account for you?"

"So I've been led to believe. But what would I do in Russia? I don't know the language and they take a singularly vicious view of my sexual orientation." He laughed.

"You'd be all right, from what I know. Artists are still held in high regard in the Soviet Union, and most laws seem to be suspended to aid and abet them. They'd give you a dacha in a Moscow suburb. Think of the theatre you might see. Aren't you curious to see a Russian production of *Streetcar*?"

"I'm told that I'm the most produced playwright in the

Soviet Union, equal to Shakespeare and Chekhov. Perhaps we should go over and organize a Tennessee Williams Festival. That would create an international media
blitz—and not all of it of a negative nature, we might
presume."

"That's one trip I would take with you, Tennessee. I can
see us flying through the snowy streets of Moscow, borne by
troikas, swathed in sable lap robes."

"I see you do have a certain largely undetected taste for
the high life. Of course, you tipped your hand with the
Maxim's party. But before we call my travel agent, let's run
through this a little more carefully. Do you think we should
attempt to spend the entire $6 million in the one trip?"

"Easily. There would be the receptions in sundry czarist
palaces for the powers that be, for the theatrical establishment. You'd be expected to supply Roederer Cristal by the
barrel."

"Roederer Cristal?"

"The champagne of the czars, Tennessee. Then you could
buy up large quantities of emeralds and bales of sable pelts
for your lady admirers back home. But give the lion's share
of the money to a foundation for a theatre school."

"Forgive me, baby, but I'm exhausted by the sheer
excellence of your proposal. I think Key West and then,
just possibly, Sicily are more within my limitations just
now. But, you're right. I should do something about that
money back in Russia."

After lunch, we went back to the theatre for a last-
minute peek at the production before it opened that night.
Gary Tucker and Schuyler Wyatt were making last-minute
adjustments to the *Moose Lodge* set. There was a prominent,
framed photograph of the son of the house who dies from
alcoholism as the play begins. The character appears in the
script only as a reference, but the picture offered just the

right touch of reality to his existence. It was of a rather good-looking, though flamboyant, gay boy.

"I think that's a good touch, Gary," I said by way of making some conversation with him.

"That's what's called a bit of business in the theatre world. It's a little touch, but it is effective."

Gary sounded both sad and sincere. As the opening neared, he must have realized that Tennessee had created a situation where Gary would be the big loser, if the critical reception of the plays was negative. Tennessee would be wounded, of course, but he already had his emotional insurance policy in the form of a contract for the production of his work in progress the next spring. That vision of Gary on the set proved symbolic. He was like an interior decorator, hired to touch up the property for a quick sale to the audience. His ambitious orchestrations, which had already cost him and Schuy so much, were now tissue-thin. And they were there upon the stage, for all to see.

The reviews the next day in the two major dailies confirmed my worst suspicious. Richard Christiansen, the drama critic for the *Chicago Tribune,* had read the situation clearly: "The presence of pain—pain of loss, pain of abandonment, pain of death—is nothing new to Tennessee Williams. But in this wintry trio, it erupts in a bleak slapstick that expresses life as a mad, pathetic farce." Of *Moose Lodge,* particularly, he observed, "These swift shifts in mood require the most delicate and skilled direction and acting, qualities that the Goodman presentations, staged by Gary Tucker, do not possess in great quantity . . . with some exceptions, emotions are flung out when they should be held back, lines are roared when they should be whispered, jokes are underlined when they should be soft-pedaled." Of *A Perfect Analysis Given by a Parrot,* he reflected that the dramatic situation would be more poignant if "the two ancient playgirls who wander into a run-down bar were not played so broadly or directed so grossly." Of the playwright's scripts, Christiansen commented, "Like many of Williams' later dramas, they are overwritten and underwritten in crucial parts."

The review in the *Chicago Sun-Times* by David Elliott switched the focus of attack away from Tucker and more onto Tennessee. He concluded his largely negative review with: *"Tennessee Laughs* is Williams whittled down: Williams becomes television."

And with this news, Tennessee and his two friends fled to Key West.

CHAPTER XX

Seance on Sunset Boulevard

THOUGH TENNESSEE'S MOTHER, EDWINA, had died the summer before, he showed little external grief, nor did he comment on her passing at any great length. She had figured, recast, in many of his great plays, beginning with her as Amanda in *Glass Menagerie* and continuing, as he frequently said, with the lobotomy-oriented Mrs. Venable in *Suddenly Last Summer.*

Those few who had remained close to him presumed that he had adjusted to her death through her long illness, when photographs sent on by Dakin revealed a mummy yet alive. "Why should I go visit a ghost?" he would say as he raised his lugubrious eyes from the latest plea for a visitation to mother from his brother.

But Tennessee's preoccupation with ghosts, which had begun with *Clothes for a Summer Hotel,* now continued in real life; it had become clear that whatever drama remained for Tennessee would be acted out, with only shreds of his last day-to-day life left as testament in those final plays.

The voice on the phone was Gary Tucker's. "Tennessee's back, Bruce. He said he lost your phone number and asked me to find you. Here he is now." It was March 15, 1981.

"At last we've landed in a hotel that knows how to treat celebrities," Tennessee laughed as he came on the phone. "In their exuberance of welcome they have given me a suite only slightly smaller in scale than San Simeon. We call it the Norma Desmond Suite. It's as heavy-handed Spanish as anything I've ever seen in the confines of Sunset Boulevard."

"I know the old Sheraton's famous for those museum-quality rooms. I've never seen them."

"But you will tonight, baby, if you'd be so kind as to indulge me in a little fantasy I have in mind. There are other guests coming at 9:00 P.M., which I specified since they're friends of Gary's; and if I had invited them any earlier, they would have expected to have been fed, you know. But could you come by about 8:00 or 8:30? I wish to speak to you privately before the party begins."

Schuy was at the door. He was much thinner than the spring before. He looked wan and almost ill.

"Are you all right, Schuy? You've dropped some weight."

"He's working us all pretty hard," said Schuy, laconically.

"What's that, baby, working you too hard am I?" Tennessee had appeared suddenly, clad in a purple kimono, from a dark corridor behind the door. Schuy jumped back and retired.

"They thought theatre was an easy life. But I'm teaching them. You either live it or you don't. Come on in to Norma's drawing room, baby. We've got some talking to do."

"You're looking well, Tennessee. The kimono's something new, at least for me."

"It defines my role, should it escape anyone's attention, baby. I've told Gary and Schuy that we're having a seance with the guests here tonight. They think it's a put-on. But I want one other person to know that it's no joke. Have you been to a seance before?"

"Never. But films have shown them often enough. So I get the gist. Isn't the idea to contact someone from the great beyond, who may then have some message of import for the living?"

"That's the general idea. I used to try them back in the sixties, after Frankie died. But experts said I had too many conflicting substances in my system for me to act as a viable channel, of any kind, I guess. But I woke up this morning and knew I had to have a seance for Edwina."

"You think your mother has something to say to you that she didn't say before she died?"

"It's my conception that she may have something to say to me, of course, but also to those around me, if you catch my drift." He was in earnest, but he chuckled warmly.

"Well, you do look rather medium-like." He had slightly curled and fluffed out his hair, which created an effective aureole above the flowing lines of the purple kimono.

"This is how we'll do it. I want everyone to sit around the low table in front of the Spanish Renaissance sofa in the great hall." He was beaming with delight that the hotel had provided him with this great stage for his performance that night.

In his usual manner, Tennessee had attempted to personalize even this vast, many-roomed suite. Hotel art deemed beyond even the redemption of camp was lowered and placed face forward against the wall. And, he had brought the tools of his own art with him, as well as a half-finished portrait of Schuyler Wyatt. It was displayed dramatically upon an easel in the entrance hall. It set the tone immediately. We were among artists.

Tennessee had retired for a bit and I was left in the company of Gary Tucker, who was puffing rather aggressively on a marijuana cigarette.

"You're seeing Tennessee in his campy form tonight, which you probably haven't seen before. Some of our nights in Key West are like this. He slips on that kimono and we put on an uncut version of a classic like *Lifeboat*. We hoot and roar at Tallulah's every line."

"But tonight I gather we're in for something different." Tennessee had cautioned me not to reveal to anyone participating in the evening's activities that he was dead serious about the seance before it began. He wanted them to anticipate a camp experience, rather than what he clearly had in mind. "Is this your first seance with Tennessee?" I asked.

"Yes. He's asked me to gather up some of my friends who helped with the production of "Tennessee Laughs." He couldn't invite them for dinner though. Just for some grass and the seance." He offered me the cigarette, but I opted for the playwright's private reserve of red wine instead.

As I wandered about the cavernous suite, I sensed that a distance had come between its occupants. Gary was not with Tennessee. Schuy was not with Gary. Tennessee was alone.

Suddenly, as I explored the suite, an arm reached from a darkened bedroom and pulled me in. Tennessee was urgent. "Remember, Bruce. These silly queens are expecting a joke. Let them continue to think so. It will make my job easier. At the table, I want you to sit at the head, on my right-hand side."

Tennessee was as serious as he was precise about his stage directions. The four new guests arrived within minutes. They were served with their drug of choice and then rushed rather unceremoniously to the table.

Immediately, it became apparent that the set was not as Tennessee had wished it. He grabbed my wrist and rose

from the table. "Gary evidently did not take my direction
seriously enough. I requested candles. We must have a
table of candles in order to perform this rite."

Gary jumped up. "I couldn't find any Tennessee. There
aren't any in the suite. I thought we could just lower the
lights." The lights were low and the magnificent twinkle of
Michigan Avenue through the three-story window below
added a kind of magical sparkle to the proceedings.

"I have delegated my last *mise en scene* to you, Mr.
Tucker," Tennessee said rather savagely. "Schuy, call room
service. Call the manager, if need be. But get those candles
up here to this suite quick."

Within an extraordinarily short time, Schuy reap-
peared, bearing a silver tray piled high with a variety of
candles. A clear plastic bag held an assortment of holders.

"Tennessee, the manager came up himself and said he
hoped these would do. We're to call immediately if you
want another kind and he'll send out for them."

"What's that manager on?" snarled Tennessee. "Where
would he send someone for candles at this improbable hour
of the night?"

Meekly, Gary and Schuy began to select candles and
place them on the table. The lights were lowered. Now, we
had the magical effect for which Tennessee had sought. The
tapers of varying lengths flickered opalescently against the
harder lights of the streets below. The lowered room lights
lent an amber glow.

Impatiently, but with the slow pace he evidently regarded as appropriate for a seance, Tennessee intoned, "Join
hands easily with your partner on either side of you. Lower
your heads. Close your eyes as softly as you can."

With obedience, the group became silent and did as they
had been directed.

"I am Astarte," Tennessee began. "Bruce, tell them who
Astarte is."

This was uncanny. We hadn't spoken of Astarte at all before the seance. But I did know, by heart, a reference to this Phoenician goddess of fertility.

"I know a verse about her from Poe, Tennessee. Should I recite it?"

He gave my hand, held in his, a slight squeeze.

"In his poem *Ulalume,* Poe says:

> *"And now, as the night was senescent*
> *And star-dials pointed to morn—*
> *As the star-dials hinted of morn—*
> *At the end of our path a liquescent*
> *And nebulous lustre was born,*
> *Out of which a miraculous crescent*
> *Arose with a duplicate horn—*
> *Astarte's bediamonded crescent*
> *Distinct with its duplicate horn."*

At that moment, I couldn't believe there could exist more perfect lines for that time and place. I certainly wouldn't have bet that I still retained those lines of verse, which I had last read some twenty years before.

Tennessee was pleased that he had had this assistance in alerting the group that his mission in this seance was far from camp.

"Astarte, spirit, you have been summoned in the form and name of mother, Edwina. We are receptive and wish to know if you have some communication for us."

The group telegraphed its tension through its linked hands.

After a moment, Tennessee spoke, hush-toned. "You wish to reveal the true state, the status, of each one here?" A pause. Then he began again. "With which member of this party will we begin?"

Before assembling, someone in the group had opened a window to help dispel the heavy marijuana smoke. A sudden breeze caused the tapered candle flames to bend towards the sofa. Tennessee began with the guest to his left. When he came to Schuy, he said, "You are one who has lost his way just as you had thought to find it. You must turn now to new directions. You will find your position false until you find your true calling. I cannot help you. I can only reveal what is true. Is music your art? Then you must make it your life. And, you must do this alone."

Tennessee and I both opened our eyes, still downcast, to see any reaction from the group. They were either attentive or simply stunned by the bald honesty of Edwina/Astarte's evaluation. Short shrift was given to the two others who were between Schuy and Gary Tucker.

At Gary, Tennessee paused and sighed deeply. He did this with great effect two or three times. Then he intoned: "At what peril do we mere humans bend our ambitions along another's path? Do you presume to know the way of the other? Paths that had passed for a time together with some degree of passion now pass divergently from one another. This is to no one's blame. There is still now time for an attempt at grace. But no human force can redirect your destiny."

Astarte knew well how to bedevil her devotees. Gary's face crumpled into confusion, then reasserted itself, to our discreet gaze, with something like contempt. Tennessee now came to me.

"Here, let me take both your hands," he said as he grasped mine in his. "My friend, you have been through hell. But as I see you now I can tell you that you will be well. That you are well. That is all you want to hear now. And your friend here knows it is enough, for he is to be believed."

In that I had been through the hell of the surgery required by the disease which had begun to manifest itself when I was with Tennessee in New York, this was indeed all I wanted or could wish to hear.

And now Tennessee rose with hands upturned in a rather Biblical gesture. "Mother, Edwina, we have come to your son now. What will you say to him? Have you a communication for him strong enough to break the bonds of death?"

We all looked up at this dramatic figure. There was a pause. And then, from Tennessee, a long drawn out "Ohhhh."

He dashed with his kimono waving about him out of the great hall and down a dark corridor. In a moment, after the opening of a door, a faint, "Here?" Then a closing of that door and a muffled movement to another. A door opening, a muffled, "Here, then?" And then again a closing door and the quiet movement to another.

Here, at the opening of the door, we could hear Tennessee say, "I see." Then the door closed behind him. After a brief moment, we could hear his muffled voice again through the door. "Mother? Is it you?" And then a high-pitched scream. A brief screech like an eagle just vanishing from sight.

Tennessee did not return for some minutes. As we rose from the table, I said to the group, "Tennessee wished me to advise you all that this seance was not a joke."

It was late in the day for that remark, but I could not resist making it.

When Tennessee returned, he had removed the kimono and wore dark slacks and a shirt.

"Who did you say Astarte was, Bruce? I'm certain I had never heard of her before I said her name tonight."

With that, he laughed warmly, hugged me, and walked me to the door.

CHAPTER XXI

An Outrageous Mask

"JUST HOW BAD DID you rate the last Goodman production?" asked Tennessee as we settled into the back room of Azteca, an Old Town Mexican restaurant which had become a kind of habit of ours because of its unpretentious merrymaking and prevailing discretion.

"My opinion was virtually the same as our critics, though I issued it somewhat in advance of their reviews. To no avail, of course."

As the piñatas glowed warmly overhead with their promise of small prizes, Tennessee ruminated about his present fate, a subject he warmed to over a plate of chili rellenos and a glass of cheap red wine.

"I'm powerless over Gary and Schuy right now, you know. I know you think I should kick them out, and I believe Greg Mosher is of the same opinion, but he is too polite—or too frightened—to say so. The important thing is that I'm writing and keeping my name as an

active playwright before the theatre-going public. I
don't see much action from the competition just now," he
cackled.

In past discussions it had been clear that he rated Arthur
Miller as a one-play writer. Of the young breed now mak-
ing theatrical headlines, he seemed to muse most about
David Mamet.

"I don't think he's gay. He's not good-looking enough.
But he has the gift of the gab. I know I shouldn't say so but
I think it's pretty ephemeral stuff."

"As I've said before, keep that under your hat. He's a
friend of Greg's and there's no need to do anything to try to
alienate his affections. He's certainly going all out for you."

"That goddamned birthday party is coming up. Can't
we stop it? I promised you I'd be at yours at Maxim's, since
the Lady Goldberg has been such a lovely hostess throughout these recent Chicago years. But you know how I feel
about uptown shit. I spend my days thinking of ways to
avoid it. If I can't, I reach for the Seconal. I just want to get
House onto the stage with a minimum of controversy and
then get back to Key West to work on *Masks Outrageous and
Obscure*. Please help me, as you have in the past, by keeping
this unpleasant aspect of the playwright's sad existence at
bay."

"I'm sorry, Tennessee, but I think you're in for it. You're
part of Greg's promotional package and he's got to deal
with that board of his. They're the ones more or less footing
the bill for this production."

"Theatres with boards of directors! A nightmare, pure
and simple! I remember all that fuss about Vanessa Redgrave, whom I am determined to have for *Masks*. Do they
think I have it out for those of the Hebrew persuasion and
that I have any power whatsoever to halt the march of
Zionism?"

"In Chicago, right now, Goodman is your temple and your book is Mamet. Really, you must be advised by this."

"Can't I just lie low? I've promised Kup I'd appear on his show, but except for that inevitable indiscretion, I won't do any press. I'm on to their game."

The evening ended on a note of some acrimony in that I had no power to dispel the inevitable gloom of the vast birthday party in the Goodman lobby for the next night.

At about eight o'clock the next night, I received a panicked call from the columnist Aaron Gold. "I know I haven't been Prince Charming with you over any of this Tennessee situation, Bruce, but please try to help us. I'm calling from the Goodman and he's still not here! Can you think of any way to get him here? Is he with you? Gary said you might be preventing his appearance."

"Don't be silly, Aaron. I spent an hour at dinner last night convincing him he should attend your gala. I presumed he was convinced, although rather unhappily so."

"Gary and Schuy are prancing around here as though the show were for them. God, how I've come to dislike them!"

"Maybe you could kill two birds with one stone by sending them to collect Tennessee and then refusing to admit the two of them when they return. That would seem to fit the style of this engagement."

"Gary and Schuy are being absolutely unprofessional. They will do nothing. Please help."

"Tennessee hates these kind of dos, Aaron. He agreed earlier on because he was negotiating for the production when the idea was proposed."

"Bruce, there are three hundred people here at the Goodman. Please get him here. I'll even forgive you for Princess Margaret!" (Nancy Goldberg, as hostess for a reception for England's Princess Margaret, had opted to have society types at the table with the princess and had seated the press at a separate table. Aaron Gold had always blamed me for Nancy Goldberg's decision.)

We both laughed at that and I agreed.

Tennessee answered his phone at the hotel with the touchingly gentle, somewhat fey manner he used when anticipating the kindness of strangers.

"It seems Goodman's giving a party, Tennessee."

"What's that, baby? Oh, I told Schuyler Wyatt to say I just wasn't up to it. I'm just too tired fighting with everyone about this increasingly-dubious mounting of my play."

"Tennessee, you do remember that I have your best interests at heart?"

"When I believe anyone has, I tend to bestow that honor upon you, baby."

"Then do us both a favor and go to that goddamned party at the Goodman."

"Those parties are part of what I used to call the catastrophe of success. I thought I'd just take the evening for a rest and some writing. I believe I see now where I can compensate for the consummate incompetence of the direction with some of my best writing. I simply must be selfish and give myself only to my writing. There's so little time."

"Tennessee, if you're a no-show tonight, you'll undo all the good we've tried to accomplish in reversing your image of the last two decades. One of the reasons you're at Goodman now is that people are taking a fresh look at you. Don't throw it away."

"I don't believe that omnipotent board you keep bringing up could just shut down the play just now, you know. They have something at risk, too."

He had gone on talking and had not hung up. That meant he was coming to accept the inevitable.

"And, Tennessee, Helen Hayes has sent on a birthday telegram to be read at the party."

"Don't push your luck, baby. It's in spite of that telegram that I'll go. I've got a wrinkled tux around here somewhere. I wish someone was here to help me into it."

"Just throw it on and go."

"Can't you just come down here and be certain that I get into that taxicab for the Goodman?"

"Sorry, Tennessee, but that I am not prepared to do."

At dawn, I rushed to the front door to seek the fruits of my labors. As I dusted the snow off the morning paper I saw that my efforts had not been in vain. There was Tennessee, wrapped rakishly in his coyote fur and sporting black tie. Goodman had got its pound of flesh.

The taping of Tennessee's only other public appearance was scheduled for that afternoon. He had agreed to appear on Kup's talk show and kept his commitment because "it will be good for the show, you know."

Tennessee's impish humor betrayed itself as he sat with his fellow guests to talk with Kup. I was alone in being vastly amused because, during the entire show, he held up, as if on display, a copy of *Sexual Perversity in Chicago,* with the author's byline visible to all. He had taken me at my word and sworn allegiance to the Mamet cause. There for the world to see was Tennessee Williams embracing David Mamet. It would prove a kind of shield for him as the interview veered into the inevitable discourse of drugs and alcohol.

"What did you think of my performance on the Kup show?" Tennessee asked with glee when he called that evening.

"Well, you played it for humor and that's about all we can hope for at this point. I'm sure your gesture eluded almost everyone, alas."

"I was sort of hoping that the audience would come to think that I really was David Mamet, after a prolonged bout with the drugs and alcohol which seem to obsess the imagination of Mr. Kupcinet."

And he had called it with the title of his new play. His masks were both outrageous and obscure.

CHAPTER XXII

―――――― ∞ ――――――

A Play Not Meant To Be

IF ONE WISHED TO summon an image with which to
briefly visualize the central defect of Tennessee's present
theatrical dilemma, one would imagine baggage from the
era of steamer trunks made to make do for the jet age. *A
House Not Meant to Stand* was an eight-character play de-
manding an amplitude of space on which to enact its
drama. Instead, *House* was given the Goodman Studio
stage again, suitable for a poetry recital or a restricted
chamber drama.

Somehow, Tennessee managed to summon an aura of
hopeful expectancy to these late Chicago doings despite the
recent catastrophic experience of "Tennessee Laughs." Persons who had wandered into and out of rehearsals began a
rumor campaign which was summed up by an anonymous
wag's "A Play Not Meant to Be."

To add to the impulsive nature of the production, Tennessee was now experimenting with broad physical gesture

as an attempted means to bring an element of laughable farce to the central message of this family tragedy. Slapstick in a Williams play was in itself alienating, but, beyond that, it was a clear and present danger to the cast, who had no room to move without occasionally lashing into one another. Tennessee's cousin Stell Adams, informed of these adventures, observed, "He was doing it all on purpose. He loved that kind of thing, to put people in false and dangerous positions." On some level, it was true that "Tennessee Laughs." Some suspected that he was laughing at the very people who were trying so valiantly, albeit with a high incidence of self-interest, to put on these last awkward plays. As has been indicated, if the sense of drama didn't work in the play, it could still be effected in real life.

Tom Biscotti, who had been stage manager for "Tennessee Laughs," wondered aloud whether the playwright "had insufficiently absorbed the fundamental stylistic tricks of "The Carol Burnett Show." Perhaps the somnolent writer only gained occasional glimpses of the action as he windowed into consciousness and so didn't get the complete picture. In any event, they're trying to do something which has already been done by professionals and I won't have anything to do with House. I just wasn't made to stand it."

In that spring mountings of new plays by Tennessee Williams were now becoming an annual event, the initial public excitement had worn off and the proceedings at the Goodman were conducted in something of a vacuum. The dynamics of the entire operation were so inverted that it all became a kind of vortex of paralysis.

Word of play production detail, often lethal to theatrical success, had leaked to writers and editors and had made their anticipation of this new play far from sanguine.

On the afternoon of opening night, Tennessee called in a

tone of some genuine anguish. "I'm certain that *House* is like that painful Southern joke of mine. Hot or cold, the corpse is going out in the morning!"

"How so, Tennessee?"

"The *Tribune's* drama critic, Christiansen, was just here at the hotel to talk to me. I wasn't in a particularly receptive frame of mind, you know, and consequently seemed to elect to forget his name. He's sure to have his revenge when he reviews the play."

"I think I can offer you some comfort there, Tennessee. Richard Christiansen is a gentleman—the last person in the world to have a grudge, let alone hold one. Curious that he stopped by, though. What did he want?"

"That was just it. I could not discover what information he came in search of, though I ultimately determined that he was there to gather material for the paper's morgue. I'm on the way out, baby, and they don't want me to forget it. And don't tell me I'm being difficult. Greg and Gold have a television crew coming to the Goodman for an interview with no announced air time. Do they think they have me completely fooled? The wool's not worth the pulling, as they should know by now."

"If you don't want to do it, just tell them to put it off. If it's publicity for the play, of course you should do it. I'll see what I can find out for you."

It seemed that Tennessee had hit the nail on the head. There was no immediate purpose for the television taping, so that time-consuming project was put off for a time.

Once again, the new Tennessee Williams play opened on his birthday, an irony which Tennessee observed as he arrived for the intimate birthday party at Maxim's de Paris that I had arranged with its owner, Nancy Goldberg.

"This will be the last one, you know. I'm checking out. But it's good to be with friends at this last, sad rite."

The guest list included close friends from the media, persons who understood Tennessee and offered him warm company. Among them was Carolyn McGuire, entertainment editor for the *Chicago Tribune,* whom Tennessee would take a great fancy to and later identify as a long-lost cousin from eastern Tennessee.

The price of Tennessee's appearance was the inclusion of Gary and Schuy on the guest list.

"I have to live it out, you know. To add recriminations about banishment from birthday parties is beyond my limited resources right now," he had said.

And so they appeared, Schuy in his guise as court minstrel, carrying his guitar case. By this time he had been rather clearly identified with Val in *Orpheus Descending* and thereby lent a rather mythic presence to the proceedings.

By this turn in their careers with Tennessee, both Gary and Schuy were clearly reduced personages and were treated with something very near contempt by the playwright.

In any event, the production of that night at Maxim's, uniting the talents of Tennessee and Gary at last in an effective drama, would be remembered by all. Few, of course, understood that the evening's proceedings were not in the least spontaneous, although to say that they had been fully or consciously preconceived would be to belittle its achievement.

The opening act of what would be a three-act, two-scene play began in the Bagatelle Room, where we had held the cast party for *Clothes for a Summer Hotel* the year before. Hardbound volumes of Tennessee's collected works were piled on the gorgeous art nouveau tables beneath the Sem cartoons. With something of a flourish, Tennessee inscribed a volume for each of the guests as a memento of what he called "packing up before checking out."

Lulled by the seeming normalcy of this gesture, the birthday dinner was announced by the maitre d'. Our table was in a private, back quadrant of the room, where we could, at the discretion of our absent hostess, carry on the celebration in what small privacy the room allowed.

It was a fine corner of the room from which to take in its architectural and design perfections. Internationally recognized as an interior masterpiece of Bertrand Goldberg, who had given the city that external landmark, Marina City, nearly as recognizable in Chicago as the Tour d'Eiffel was in the City of Light.

Gathered closely at the table, we were eight. Champagne was poured. Then, Tennessee placed one hand in mine, the other in Carolyn's. He looked upward at the belle epoque sconces, which lent subtle and theatrical lighting to our group. For a moment, I feared another seance.

"This is quite some place," he said. Then, he held up a piece of folded white paper. Had he prepared a commemorative poem for the occasion?

He intoned in his reverberant French: "Saucissons et Terrines du Chef (dramatic pause); Consumme de Homard au Gingembre (dramatic pause); Pithivier de Ris Veau et d'Escargots (great emphasis); Sorbet au Pamplemousse rouge (lightly, en passant); Canard roti Rouenaise avec sa garniture (gravelish intonation); Gratin de Framboise (a tone of resolve); Cafe (flourish, full stop)."

He had run through the whole recital before anyone quite grasped that he was reading from the evening's commemorative menu. Nonetheless, the reading was received with due appreciation, which it surely deserved to be. It was a masterly reading.

"I wished to do honor to our hostess, who, though of unparalleled generosity to a writer not in his first bloom, remains a woman of some mystery in that she never pre-

sents herself at these gatherings. I remember meeting the
lady at our cast party for *Clothes;* but, though her presence
in person is regrettably absent, her grace is all about us.
I've told Bruce that she's our Madame von Meck, you know.
The woman who backed Tschaikovsky without inflicting
her company on that tortured soul."

Now into the "Saucissons et Terrine du Chef" and the
Chablis Grand Cru, Albert Pic, this musical reference
seemed to provide Gary Tucker with a cue. He rather
brusquely pushed Schuyler from his seat as encouragement
to begin his phase of the evening's entertainment. Schuy
retired to an adjacent banquette to open his guitar case,
removed the glittering guitar and strapped it over his
shoulder. Quite beautiful and blond, he returned to the
table and began to sing:

> *"Starry, starry night*
> *Paint your palette blue and gray . . ."*

It was "Vincent," Don McLean's anthem to Van Gogh,
which was played everywhere at the time. In the manner of
parties, few at first attended to the words. But they could
not be dismissed. The song went on:

> *". . . Portraits hung in empty walls,*
> *Frameless heads in nameless halls*
> *With eyes that watch the world and can't forget."*

The beautiful, sensitive hymn went on and Schuy was
giving it all he had. But the effort was beginning to tell.
His voice began to thin, even to tremble as he came to the
crucial verse:

> *"Now I think I know what you tried to say to me*
> *How you suffered for your sanity*

How you tried to set them free.
They would not listen.
They did not know how.
Perhaps they'll listen now."

It was a heady scene, wrapped as we were in the opulent warmth of belle epoque Maxim's, attended by this sudden incarnation of Apollo who was giving the words to the song a kind of Delphic resonance.

". . . I could have told you, Vincent
This world was never meant for one as beautiful as you.
Starry, starry night . . .
Weathered faces, lined with pain,
Are soothed beneath the artist's loving hands."

At these words, Schuy began to weave and to fall backwards. One of our guests, David Dolson, a feature editor at the *Tribune,* gallantly rose to catch him in his fall. He pulled himself together and left the room.

Tennessee looked about rather deeply and said, "Hm-mmmmm," an utterance usually meant to signify the capture and filing of a usefully emotional dramatic event.

Having witnessed this exhausting redemption of Schuy's, we proceeded with the party, which Tennessee enlivened with warm anecdotes of amusing theatrical events.

Two scenes. Three acts. It was the quintessential Williams of 1981.

CHAPTER XXIII

---◦◦◦---

Gulag in Paradise

IN THE ECLIPSE OCCASIONED by the fall of *The House Not Meant to Stand,* Tennessee retired to Key West with his two play fellows and there pursued the island game of wine, sun, sleep, and sex. This being the time-proven formula for recovery from the exacerbations of ill-favored play productions.

But now, in November 1981, the words from Key West came darker. The menage at the Duncan Street house was regrouping in its further descent into this hell of their own making. For a time, Tennessee preserved the notion of love and support for his Orphic Schuy and lipservice to the directorial talents of Gary Tucker. But only for the briefest of times.

The Duncan Street complex was in four primary parts. There was the main, small white house; between the living room and the kitchen there was an exit to the palm-shaded pool; in the back of the property were the small outbuild-

ing in which Tennessee would write and then a kind of
shed. That shed had become, in more than one instance, a
spot of last resort for companions of the playwright.

In its last sad use, the shed had become the last refuge of
Robert Carroll, a beautiful, talented young man who was
one of Tennessee's friends in the late 70's. It is the acrylic
portrait of Carroll which illustrates the dust jacket of
Tennessee's last book of poems, *Androgyne, Mon Amour.*

Tennessee had a rather touching regard for this young
man, who had now long vacated the shed to which his
destiny with Tennessee had bound him. When Tennessee
and I were in New York for *Clothes,* letters would arrive
from the unfortunate young man—full, Tennessee said,
"of some of the best writing in the country today. I support
him for his talent though I can ill afford the two hundred a
week I now have the attorneys send to him on a regular
basis. But he is paralyzed. Physically paralyzed. He must
lie upon hard floor boards because his back gives him such
agony. None of the usual painkillers will help him. It is in
this pain that he writes these letters to me. They must cost
him exquisite pain to do so."

These letters, which were never shared, had as their
point of origin a state in the South, to which Carroll had
fled in late 1979, just before I met Tennessee. How he had
managed to pull himself from the enclosure in the back of
Tennessee's garden is something of a mystery.

Tennessee had informed cousin Jim that "Robert's re-
form has collapsed. He has now retired to the garden shed,
leaving word that he will not present himself for either
lunch or dinner and that should I wish to communicate
with him, I must do so with notes addressed to a box at the
main post office. I must try to get him out of there and to
Tangier. He has friends of a kind nature there, and there is
plenty of grass, called kif in those parts."

In his despair, Carroll had painted the interior walls of the garden shed black. There he slept and drugged and shunned the company of his former lover. That he soon substituted South Carolina for Tangier is in the tradition of the playwright's promise.

When Tennessee and his entourage arrived back in Key West in the happy guise of what Key West lore called "The Williams family," there was an accompanying sense of ruin for the two young people, who now realized they had exhausted the potential of their association with Tennessee.

A strange and rather urgent call from Tennessee alerted me to the situation.

"Couldn't you come on down here for your long-postponed trip to an island in the sun? You always look better with a tan, baby. That much I can promise you. It's warm and sunny down here, if we speak of the area immediately beyond the confines of this Duncan Street property."

"Things aren't going well at the house, Tennessee?"

"I have learned now, permanently, I hope, that I may stand in no further need of education, that charm can be a most dangerous human weapon. I speak of Schuyler Wyatt, of course. His falsity has now become apparent. I have given him a motor scooter as a practical means of getting about the island. It seems now that that vehicle, so innocent in appearance as it sits in front of the house, is bearing him out of my life."

"Well, amen to that then, Tennessee. I know it sounds callous, but it was inevitable, wasn't it?"

"But that's just the point, baby. Why do things always have to end so badly? And I can't get them to leave. Gary Tucker has completely given up on trying to achieve any compatibility in the situation, which is beset with diffi-

culties. I try not to ignore them when I see them, but I
must get on with my writing, you know. They seem not to
respect my most fundamental requirements."

"Then isn't it time to just call it quits?"

"I don't think they'll leave of their own volition, baby.
Gary's appropriated the garden shed that used to house
Robert Carroll. In this heat, it must be like a Javanese
torture hut, but still he lives there. And Schuyler treats my
house as casually as a college dormitory, as though I have
maintained this home at such great expense merely for his
occasional comfort."

Tennessee's invitation to join this dark domestic arrangement was easily dismissed.

"I'm sorry you're having a bad time, Tennessee. Are you
able to get on at all with your writing? Have you recovered
from the Goodman *House?*"

"I learned a lot from this last go around. I haven't given
up on *House,* you know. There's plenty of dark humor and
some of my best writing in recent years. You know Greg
Mosher has promised another mounting, this time on the
main stage, so I feel as heartened about the immediate
future as I possibly can."

"You do know that Goodman won't tolerate another
Tucker production, don't you?"

"That's why I have to get them out of here. I don't want
them to know what I'm doing with this script. Their
intermittent interest in it is pathetic, you know. Can't you
just come down for a few days, perhaps a nice, long
weekend? I know we could handle this somewhat delicate
situation with appropriate equanimity."

"Eviction isn't in my line, Tennessee. But you have
another great friend who would relish the role. Why not
call on Maria to help?"

"Maria St. Just! I never thought to hear you name her

again! You think I should call her from London at enormous expense to help me kick a couple of kids out into the street? No sir. It will be the police! I see now that I must call the police! They'll oblige me, as they have in the past when the situation has become a little too intense."

"Tennessee, I really think you should stop short of calling the cops. I mean, just how humiliating for everyone must this get? If you're really tired of the arrangement, pension them off for a while. I'm sure if they had the means to live elsewhere they would go quietly."

"You think I have endless funds for this purpose? They've both been on my payroll for almost two years now! And you speak of a pension!"

"You set up a relief fund for Robert Carroll. Why not set up something for these two? It needn't go on forever. Just give them some breathing time."

"I see now that I've set a dangerous precedent with Robert. I had hoped no one would ever know about the arrangement."

"I'm offering you the easiest, least traumatic option, Tennessee. You have the money. You may remember the disclosure at the Eastman office."

"I'll never do it! Never! They've had all they're going to get from me."

"Well, maybe your new friend, that black minister, can counsel you. He seemed quite proprietary when last I talked to him."

"I gave him my private number, you know. He's called me several times. He thinks a visit to the spirit world would ease my anxieties."

"Well, the contemporary psychiatric wisdom seems to be that whatever helps helps. I'm glad if he can make you feel better."

"So I gather I may not depend upon your help in my

present plight? I thought you might be interested in putting Gary and Schuy to rest, considering your opinion of
them."

"It's too late now. If I could have helped you see the
mistake of involving them in your Goodman productions, I
would have done anything necessary, including calling the
cops. But it's all over now, as far as I'm concerned. In truth,
I just feel sorry for them."

"Well, if I wish to jeopardize their sanity any further, I'll
pass on your newfound compassion to them. I plan a trip to
Sicily a little later in the year. Does that other island
intrigue you at all?"

"Sure, Tennessee. Let's talk more about it as the time for
your trip nears."

"I'm an old man, so I must take what I can. I hope to see
you soon, perhaps back in Chicago. There is much to do for
the new production, including the selection of a new director for *House*. Perhaps we can look at the prospect a bit
more brightly at that time."

Rumor from the island soon reached Chicago. Tennessee
had taken a more humane approach to his riddance of his
two charges. Shortly after our talk, he took Gary and Schuy
to meet David Wolkonsky, the Key West real estate devel-
oper, who had recently opened The Sands, a posh resort on
the Atlantic shores of the island. It was his policy to
employ gay personnel almost exclusively, and so Tennessee
found Wolkonsky in a receptive mood when he told him he
would be in his debt if he would find some employ for Gary
and Schuy.

Gary was given the job of "celebrity DJ" at the pier at
the Sands, where he played a ragged mix of reggae and rock
to the heavily-sedated crowd which frequented the place.
Tennessee had done Gary yet another good turn and sup-
plied him with a new stage upon which to deploy his

considerable talents. And, the introduction of Schuy to Wolkonsky set Schuy up for a lucrative career as well. Soon Schuy would disappear for weeks on end, often returning from distant parts attired in a mink or in an entire wardrobe of new and expensive clothing. He had made his metier profitable.

One day Rudolph Nureyev appeared on the pier with Tennessee in tow. Tennessee, despite the ninety-degree heat of the island, always appeared now dressed in clothes for a winter hotel, namely, his coyote parka. They both took to the shade, where Tennessee introduced his former protegees to the great legend. The introduction was not a great success in that Nureyev allegedly allowed, "As yet, I've never had to pay for it."

Under Tennessee, these two astonishing opportunists had painted themselves into an excruciating corner, one hiding out almost comatose in a black womb at the end of a tropical garden, the other fleeing as often as possible upon his motor scooter in the search for a trade with which to buy his escape. With his introduction of Gary and Schuy to Wolkonsky, Tennessee had effected his freedom and could now bring down the curtain on this particularly messy little drama, for, as soon as they had some cash in hand, they moved on to sunnier rooms.

And when next I heard from him, on the verge of yet another visit to Chicago, he seemed once again renewed.

As an engaging postscript to his call to me before he came back to Chicago, he said, "I do care for you, Bruce, with purity and appreciation and, I trust, understanding. Let's see more of each other this go around."

CHAPTER XXIV

A Diagnosis From
the Brothers Grimm

CLEANSING THE AUGEAN STABLES on Duncan Street in Key West seemed to have a reviving effect on Tennessee. He was in an ebullient mood when I next saw him in Chicago. In that time he had since visited the University of British Columbia at Vancouver. That had been an adventure of immense complications, which he was eager to share with me.

"I've had my first honest lay in years in Vancouver. A smooth-skinned youth submitted to the laying on of hands—nothing else. A sweet student at the university where I had come to lecture.

"I was seized with impenetrable gloom and foreboding early on in the lectureship, you know. I just had to get away. So I left in the middle of the night, leaving most of my belongings, and fled to San Francisco. For a solid week I stayed in bed at the hotel watching soap operas and ordering everything from room service. Then I was as suddenly seized with guilt, packed my few things and returned to

Vancouver. I gather they hadn't taken kindly to my mysterious disappearance, so I had been written out of the script
in my unexplained absence.

"I found solace in Vancouver not only in the blissful lay I
had but in the signing on of a new paid companion. He's an
amazing six-foot-eleven and possesses a sort of heartbreaking quality. Our attachment is totally sexless, but it is a
real attachment. Nevertheless, be that as it may, Miss
Winemiller will sing La Golondrina this side of the Orient,
which is my ultimate destination."

We were back at our little Mexican restaurant, where the
lights were low and the music only sporadic and discreet.
The snug tables were ideal for intimate conversation,
which was what Tennessee was definitely in the mood for.
He was more ardently articulate than I had seen him in
recent times and was in Chicago for the negotiations for the
main stage production of *A House Not Meant to Stand*.

"We're home free now, baby. Tucker and Wyatt have
revealed their true colors to me and I have banished them
from Duncan Street. Now perhaps *House* has a fighting
chance here at the Goodman."

"I'm glad you're no longer smitten with that disastrous
pair, Tennessee. That alone should make it easier for you to
work more effectively on the new production. Are you or
Greg going to choose the new director?"

"Greg has chosen a Belgian. His resume gives him a
good repute. I suppose I shall have to teach him how talk is
talked in Pascagoola. And, with the right Bella, this new
production done right, on the main stage, should reveal to
your two morning critics that these final works of mine are
better than they know."

Tennessee had removed his dark glasses and reached
across the table in a gentle manner to take my hand. He
looked younger. His face had a fresh, open appearance.

"You're looking wonderful, Tennessee. Have you been to Switzerland for those Noel Coward injections?"

"Don't think I don't remember how ill-favored you find injections, baby. But the truth is both simpler, yet more painful. I went to Houston with a local lady of Schweppes tonic wealth who is called Texas Kate. I suppose she's my closest friend in town since she has only confided her true age to me. She is fifty-six but on good days and nights can pass for a fast thirty-five."

"Yes, Tennessee, I remember, I met her at the pre-opening party in New York. She was the only decent person there. I'm glad you're still in touch with her."

"Well this thirty-fivish look of hers is not achieved by virtuous living. She has, of course, recourse to cosmetic surgery. She persuaded me to have a job done on the wrinkles about my eyes."

There was a dramatic pause as Tennessee looked earnestly at me and then quickly away, towards the ceiling, as though banishing some painful memory.

"It was the most excruciating physical pain of my life since the old son of a bitch who did it did not even give me a local anesthesia!"

"You lay there in the operating room without benefit of any kind of painkiller? It's hard to believe!"

"I can only say, believe it, baby. But you think it did me some good? Can you tell something was done?"

"As you may have noted, my reaction when you took off your glasses was unprompted. You look great."

"Then my search for some androgynous, smooth-skinned creature may be made easier. I ordered my new paid companion, whom you will meet at lunch tomorrow if you are free to do so, to find such a creature for me. I expect some resistance, in that I told him I'd pay this person two hundred a session, which is what I pay him on a weekly basis."

"I'm glad you've found someone to take care of you, Tennessee. What's his name?"

"He's Saskatch! Just Saskatch! I found him in Vancouver and I know a true Saskatch when I see one."

"What's your schedule like while you're here?"

"I'm to meet the Belgian director, Andre Ernotte by name, and see if he's got what it takes, although I'm pretty certain there's not much I can do about it if he doesn't, in my opinion. Greg and Goodman are being good to me, but I have come to know just how far I can stretch their tolerance. But on the matter of Bella I am adamant. There must be a new Bella!"

"Greg must be glad you've got Tucker out of your hair. Have you heard much from him?"

"He sent me a beautifully-typed copy of *A House Not Meant to Stand*. As it stands now it is a dark and beautiful work with plenty of humor in it. Rehearsals start March 23rd and I am to be given another birthday party three days later, but an intimate one, thank God."

The snow which had come to mark Tennessee's early winter visits to Chicago came to fall again. We were waiting for Saskatch by the Art Institute on Michigan Avenue. We were embarking on an urgent mission.

"If that Saskatch doesn't show up soon we'll just have to go to the pharmacy without him. I need these prescriptions filled immediately. I asked him to do it for me, but he seems helpless on any of the subtler levels of civilization."

A seven-foot figure, blurred in the heavy snow, was hurrying through the crowds towards us.

"That must be Saskatch, Tennessee. Now we can get going on this mission of yours."

Indeed, Saskatch looked like a person from another place and time, almost another millennium. I could see why Tennessee had referred to his heartbreaking quality.

In introducing us, Tennessee said, "You'll have to pass muster with Bruce here. You'll have to toe the line. He doesn't have much patience with my companions, if recent history is any example."

Saskatch and I laughed it off. Actually, I was relieved by what I could determine in this brief meeting. Saskatch seemed sensitive and almost certainly had no ambitions for a career on the stage. He seemed genuinely concerned about Tennessee's welfare.

As we walked with great purpose towards the pharmacy I had identified as being the closest, just over on Wabash, Saskatch told me something of his meeting with Tennessee in Vancouver and of a problem they had encountered there.

"One night at dinner," he said, "Tennessee suddenly doubled up with pain. He couldn't even speak. We rushed from the restaurant into a cab and I took him to the only doctor I knew would be available at that hour of the night. He is a German doctor of great local reputation. I felt safe to take Tennessee to him."

"It was my heart! My heart!" chimed in Tennessee as we pushed on through the snow. "That German doctor had no English and I have only rudimentary German. Saskatch has none. So there we were. After an interminable examination with no medication to relieve the symptoms, he had me dress and await his leisure in the receiving room of his office. It was the dead of night and I really thought the jig was up. The pain didn't lessen and my heart began to palpitate wildly."

"Tennessee really was in pretty bad shape," Saskatch offered as we neared the pharmacy.

"After a wait that left me nearly dead from fright, we were summoned to the great doctor's sanctum sanctorum," said Tennessee as he eagerly continued the saga. " 'I can only give you your diagnosis in idiomatic German,' he

pronounced. Then he rolled off three minutes of incompre-
hensible jargon replete with rolling eyes and steep frowns."

"Tell him what you finally said to shut him up, Tennessee," said Saskatch, opening the door to the pharmacy.

"I could endure what sounded like a death sentence
being handed down from a medieval German judge no
longer. I stood up and said: 'Clearly you believe in what
you're saying to me, but if I interpret aright all this
rigmarole sounds like a list of the titles of the more obscure
tales of the Brothers Grimm. Now is there a diagnosis
which will allow a prescription to alleviate this condition or
must I seek emergency treatment at the nearest hospital,
where I will certainly share my experience here with the
experts there?' "

The three of us were laughing rather wildly as we came
into the pharmacy, where, as it happened, the ancient
pharmacist recognized Tennessee in his coyote parka instantly.

"Tennessee Williams! My favorite playwright! Can it be
you?" All about him bubbled those glass urns filled with
Kool Aid colors, which used to declare the presence of a
pharmacist on the premises. Interspersed between those
bottles were large tanks of leeches, all in exuberant good
health.

"We've come to the right place," Tennessee said cheerily,
as he reached into his parka pocket for a sheaf of prescriptions. "I can tell you are a consummate pharmacist," allowed Tennessee with a dramatic and encompassing glance
at the room's accouterment. "I trust I may then have these
filled within the hour?"

The pharmacist was counting the prescriptions rapidly.
"There are eighteen prescriptions here, Mr. Williams. I'm
afraid . . . but no, you shall have them in less than an hour!
While you wait here, if you wish! For you I will put all else

aside and tend to this immediately. My wife will not believe you came in here! This is really something!" And he disappeared behind the glass partition to go to work.

As the pharmacist finished each prescription, he would place the bottle proudly on the counter for Tennessee to examine. Soon the full complement of eighteen bottles was before us.

Taking it all in, I said, "That should get you through the night, Tennessee!"

"Somewhere between two and three this morning there might be a need for still something more," he said, laughing. Saskatch carried this chemistry set back to the hotel.

With his pills and the understanding that he could have a new Bella, Tennessee left the snows of Chicago the very next day.

"See you in March, unless you want to come to Sicily with me next month. You may consider the invitation as always on, you know."

He would go to Sicily with Saskatch. I did not see him again until the latest incarnation of *A House Not Meant to Stand* was to open. It was to be the last production of a new play in his lifetime.

CHAPTER XXV

The Crocodile Takes a Streetcar

RELIABLE RUMOR HAD TENNESSEE pretty much on the Atlantic Ocean beach in Key West, clad in his coyote parka, throughout the fall of 1981 and into the spring of 1982. I hadn't heard much from him before a lengthy letter in February of that year, but learned that his faithful Saskatch, all seven feet of him, lay stretched beside him in the sands.

This respite was therapeutic, for he was in fine shape when he arrived in Chicago to begin rehearsals for the main stage production of *A House Not Meant to Stand*.

"I've brought us a new Bella!" he beamed triumphantly as he came from his plane in early April 1982. "Now we can show those morning critics of yours what kind of a play *House* is. I haven't met that Belgian director yet, but Greg assures me he gets the message. He's done Beckett, you know."

"He's prouder of his Shakespeare," I said. "At least that's

what he keeps talking about to the media. He did an interesting *Richard III* at Stratford with Viveca Lindfors and Michael Moriarty. What a relief that you're once more among the professionals!" It seemed like a nightmare dispelled that the Tucker era was over and that two real theatre professionals were willing and enthusiastic about *House.*

The second professional was Peg Murray, an old Tennessee veteran, who had worked with him in his *Small Craft Warnings.*

"Peg's Bella! I heard her read and she's got the accent and the darkly-humorous mood of *A House Not Meant to Stand.* We'll have to flesh her out a bit, because Bella's got that heartbreaking weight problem, but Peg's into the craziness. She'll do it!"

As we rode in from the airport, I told him that there was an interesting new production of *A Streetcar Named Desire* running in Chicago. Its director, Robert Falls, based on my viewing of the play, seemed a perfect Williams interpreter. It was obvious he worked well with women, and they seemed to be the main problem in realizing the intent of his later plays. I urged Tennessee to join me at Wisdom Bridge, where it was in performance. If he had a kind of "director-in-residence" he might be able to realize the production and performance of his plays with less trauma and so with greater success.

"But I've seen *Streetcar* so many times, baby. I know I'm just an old yard dog of a playwright, but you can't just drag me to every production you think might interest me."

"This isn't just any production, Tennessee. It's received excellent notices. I thought it might bolster your flagging feelings about Chicago audience reception to your works."

"Do they do a Sunday matinee? It's a long play and I find afternoons are best for long plays, at least at my time of life."

"I'm sure Falls will arrange for some good house seats. Sunday is firm, then?"

"We'll see *Streetcar* and go on to an early dinner. I want to fill you in on what's going on." A tantalizing cryptogram. I looked forward to Sunday, since Tennessee was back in his old good form.

I called Robert Falls at Wisdom Bridge to tell him the good news that I was bringing the great playwright to the theatre the coming Sunday.

"We'll pour champagne. We'll have a lovely little reception in the lobby. This will be wonderful." So Falls welcomed the news.

In that Tennessee had been meeting with the Goodman forces in the intervening days between our meeting and the Sunday of the play, I could only expect some retrogression. I called him on the Saturday night before the matinee.

"I hear the production is not quite what you cracked it up to be, baby. Maybe we should just forego what might be an embarrassing situation and have an early dinner instead. I have my writing and need all the time I can spare for it."

"Have you considered the source of the negative news on the Wisdom Bridge *Streetcar*?"

"I'll admit you have a point there. I asked Greg about it and he was rather cold, which is only to be expected. Theatre jealousies are dirt common. One of the kids who works the stage says Falls worries more about his groceries than his productions. Does that mean he has a condition something like our Bella?"

"The bitching just goes on and on, doesn't it? I've never seen Falls in the flesh, so I have no idea whether he's fat or not. I wouldn't think it would matter. I think he's sensitive to your writing and he might work out for you."

"Well, in the matter of directors, I like Andre Ernotte and think he'll do well by *House*. Of course, he doesn't have a clue to the way people talk in Mississippi, but he seems willing to take my word for it. But you're right. I don't think he's it for the long term. He seems to favor Paris and Belgium and I'm in no condition to make a move like that just now, you know."

"That's why Falls seems a natural to me. He's in Chicago and he understands your plays. But you'll see for yourself tomorrow afternoon. You will go?"

"There won't be dancing in the streets, will there? I mean, no Goodman-style parties?"

"There's no mood and no budget for that kind of thing at Wisdom Bridge, Tennessee. They'll pour some champagne at intermission and that will be it. You'll meet Falls and see what you think."

"Where is this Wisdom Bridge of yours?"

"It's nothing fancy. It's on the second story of a building next to the L tracks on the north side. Shall we meet in front of the theatre?"

"Okay, baby. But I rely on you to supply an exit of discreet escape if it isn't all it's cracked up to be."

It was that kind of bright, cold March day that sets all personal anxieties into high relief. Tennessee was pacing morosely before the theatre when I arrived to meet him.

Right under the L tracks, next to the door of the theatre, was a little neighborhood bar. As I caught up with him, Tennessee was heading more towards that destination than the theatre door as he paced back and forth.

"I think I could use a touch of the grape, you know. I won't get any writing done now anyway. Do we have time for a glass of wine?"

It was one of those small, dark neighborhood bars that big cities seem to offer as an immediate dose of intimacy to confront the cold realities of the outside world. As we sat at the bar, he was stroking his beard.

"I've been thinking about your Chicago theatre, baby."
"I didn't know you had seen any but your own, Tennessee."

"Seen? No. But your theatre world here seems so straight and stuffy. Mamet's not good looking enough to be gay. Falls they say is fat. I suppose this is the onslaught of democracy, you might say. I suppose it's for the best. But couldn't there be just a touch of what used to be called, rather hopelessly, glamor, a little more of an easy flight of fantasy?"

"Have you forgotten? We're the city of big shoulders, hog butcher to the world. That's sufficient for most. Meat and potatoes. Leave us alone. A nip at the end of the day. TV. Football. You know, America."

"America, courtesy, baby, of Stanley Kowalski. They got a good-looking hunk playing Stanley upstairs?"

"Good old Midwestern stock, Tennessee. He's good. Looks the part."

Obviously, Tennessee was moving into his Blanche mode in preparation for *Streetcar*. Like her, he was finding the world cold and needed a hunk and a flight of fancy.

"I think this trip will be it, baby. Unless *House* makes it, I can't very well come back here again. We've done everything we can to get this play right. I have to do all I can with Christiansen and—why does her name escape me? There must be an honest courtship. Critics are not frequently won over by anything but, what? A reading? Poetry or brief and best prose?"

"I think the critics are with you as much as they can be. They would delight in a success for you. Why not? You've been a hero of the theatre for decades. They'd love to see you come through with a triumph."

"I pray, you know. Not for schoolchild favors and benedictions, but to God in a general way. I believe the process of prayer is a great solace to humanity. Is it true God is dead? No. Against all evidence to the contrary, I feel his presence and the tender grace of Our Lady."

And on that note he finished his wine and we went up to the play.

One of the great virtues of a production like the one Wisdom Bridge was giving *Streetcar* is that lack of resources demand that the actors make the words sing. The language conveys enough imagery and *mise en scene* to carry the play meaningfully to the audience.

When Tennessee saw the set, he chuckled. "That's the ticket. Imagination!" The stage was bare of almost everything.

"Hmmmmmm," said Tennessee as Stanley came on the stage in emblematic tee-shirt to call the play's opening lines: "Hey, there! Stella, baby!"

I could tell he approved of Stanley. And the play progressed with a great sense of possession of the text. Tennessee was giving it his full attention. I felt relief that this had been a good bet. Perhaps the Falls thing would work out after all.

But the trouble started as soon as Blanche came on the stage. When she came to say: "This—can this be—her home?" the laughter began. Admittedly that could easily be interpreted as an amusing line and the audience followed the playwright's suit. They tittered loyally.

At the point of her reunion with her sister Stella, Blanche says: "Open your mouth and talk while I look around for some liquor! I know you must have some liquor on the place! Where could it be, I wonder?"

Tennessee nudged me sharply. "Can you imagine? 'Where can it be?' She saw that liquor bottle first thing!" Mutual laughter.

Blanche explains why she's off from her teaching job so

early in the semester: ". . . Mr. Graves . . . he suggested I take a leave of absence. I couldn't put all of those details into the wire."

Tennessee nudged me again. "Couldn't put those details into a wire! The services won't carry information of that kind. Screwing those underaged kids!" Warm cackling.

During her first confrontation with Stanley, he holds up the depleted liquor bottle, commenting: "Liquor goes fast in hot weather. Have a shot?" Blanche replies: "No, I never touch it."

A great guffaw from Tennessee. "She rarely touches it! Ha!"

Still, the audience, though palpably nervous, obliged him with occasional supportive titters. After all, there was visible humor in his commentary.

But the cackling, laughing, and guffawing formed an irritating counterpoint through the balance of the play. As it winds down into the denouement of Blanche's tragedy, she begins to become completely undone. She says: "How about taking a swim, a moonlight swim at the old rock quarry?" She's dressed in her faded ball gown and rhinestone tiara.

Again the nudge. "Take a swim! She's on the way to an asylum for the insane. Pretty poor sense of direction, wouldn't you say?" Titter. Laugh.

Despite the distraction of the author's amused commentary, the power of the play was pulling the audience right along. And the more they were caught up in it, the more they wanted to hear what the actors spoke. They came to resent the incessant obligato of barely-suppressed laughter.

For the champagne reception, Tennessee sat in state and obliged those bold enough to approach him with autographs and genial chatter.

As we descended the steep stairs to the street, he said, "It's one of the best productions of that play I've seen. You were right about Falls. Let's set up a meeting. Now for a glass of red wine—Blanche always makes me thirsty. Can't think why."

We went back to the little neighborhood place beneath the L tracks. The word of his presence must have spread back up to the theatre, because the bartender suddenly handed me the phone.

"Do you think you could keep Mr. Williams there for another ten or fifteen minutes? The cast would love to come down and meet with him." I turned to Tennessee. "This place is good enough for a second glass of wine, okay?" He nodded his assent.

Soon the cast came pushing through the doors, scripts in hand for the author's autograph.

Tennessee couldn't tell the cast often enough how much he loved their production. And they couldn't tell him often enough how much they loved him.

Tennessee didn't stick around for just a glass of wine. He stayed for three hours of fun, lively stage talk, something he must have sorely missed in his recent theatrical associations.

These people were the real thing. This was genuine theatre. Unadorned and irrepressibly alive.

And that Sunday evening in the bar under the L tracks was the last time for Tennessee.

CHAPTER XXVI

A Diversion by Magritte

ON THE OCCASION OF its first incarnation, Tennessee had written of *A Streetcar Named Desire* that it was composed because "only in his work can an artist find reality and satisfaction, for the actual world is less intense than the world of his invention and consequently his life, without recourse to violent disorder, does not seem very substantial."

Tennessee's recourse to disorder was now the order of the day, as his search for the substantiality of life could only now be found in his personal life. The violence was of an emotional cast, rather than physical. It became apparent that he was enacting the drama of his life through the casting of actual persons who could be instantly motivated, spurred on, and then destroyed with all the dispatch of a truly effective avenging angel. Recent history proved this.

Because of his ongoing thesis that life was inevitably tragic, he could not be personally held to account for the destructiveness of his personal life. Persons entered into his circle of their own accord and thereby participated in their own undoing.

"Security is a kind of death," Tennessee would assure his obliging victims. "The struggle is all."

In the final version of the play that was now about to open at the Goodman, *A House Not Meant to Stand,* Tennessee had worked into its fabric all that now concerned him, persons as well as issues. When I reviewed the new script for the play, I was brought up short.

I called Tennessee at his hotel. "Tennessee, I see there's a new character in *House,* one Bruce Lee Jackson, an officer of the law, it would seem. I don't believe you know any other Bruces, right?"

"Now don't you go getting all huffy with me, baby. You mind particularly being put on the side of law and order?"

"It's just that I know how you render your daily life into this play and I was bemused to find myself characterized in this way. I realize it's not a literal description, but I guess I can figure out how I got there."

"It's the view of many of my theatrical associates, you know. You seem to frighten some of them. Of course, I may have had a slight hand in that. They do know that I defer to you to an extent. And, when necessary, I haven't held back on that book, you know. Consider Officer Bruce Lee Jackson a reminder to the rest. Between us, there's nothing really similar but the name. Although now that I think of it, the role. . . ." We both laughed.

The opening night became an operatic crescendo of activity. There was the performance of the play itself. That would be followed by the long-delayed NBC taping of an interview with Tennessee, and that would then be followed by a late dinner meeting between Tennessee and Robert Falls. Tennessee was compressing all he could into as tight a time frame as possible. Applying the brush of torture to his associates at Goodman, he had been certain to tell them of his meeting with Falls.

At the intermission, columnist Aaron Gold came up to me. "You've done it again. How can you bring Falls into the picture now? Greg has done his best for Tennessee here at Goodman. Why would you want to introduce him to another director?"

"Ernotte is a one shot for this play. If Tennessee is going to continue writing and producing plays the least the community to which he has given so much can do is to provide him with all the professional backup it can. I want to prevent another Tucker/Wyatt situation. Don't you think that was embarrassing enough for everyone? I really believe that if Tennessee associated himself with a professional who was not emotionally involved with him he could move on in his development. I'm tired of all of you treating him like an invalid. It only adds fuel to the fire. I know from personal experience that if you cut through all the media crap of the last decade he's still inside there and still wants to do some good work. This Goodman thing almost worked. But the fatal flaw was the admission of Tucker to the project. Instead of spending your time trying to deny me access to Tennessee, you might have addressed yourself to the real problem, which I have been trying to solve. I want Tennessee to be able to leave this inevitable flop with some hope for the future. I think that an association with Falls might provide that hope."

Aaron listened attentively to this little tirade of mine. "Greg is furious. You mustn't tell him that I told you this, but he's going to try to see that the NBC taping goes on as late as possible so that Tennessee won't make his meeting with you and Falls tonight."

"Do you have any idea what a royal pain in the ass all of

you are? You're all acting like petty children. I know you engineered the NBC taping, which Tennessee loathes. You think that you've hoodwinked him into thinking that the taping is some kind of promotion for the play. He knows it isn't. He knows it's for the NBC morgue. You can imagine how he feels about all of you, here on opening night, pinning him down for an interview that he knows will only be aired after his death."

"You didn't have to tell him it was an obit."

"That's where you people have missed your mark. You automatically assume that because of his drinking he doesn't know what's going on. Let me assure you he does. He's going into that interview with his eyes open and he'll give it his best shot; he knows it's part of the imagery of his last years and he's still, believe it or not, concerned about the image that will be left behind."

"I believe you do care, Bruce, but all of this is beyond anybody's control now. I don't know that Tennessee will ever get to your meeting with Falls tonight because you won't be able to do anything about it. You've been banned from the set."

"Thanks for telling me, Aaron. I'll just have a word with him before he goes into the studio. I think you've backed the wrong horse, Aaron, but I understand how it's happened that you did so. Thanks for letting me in on the plot."

Despite all its burnishing and expansion to the full-blown main stage at the Goodman, *A House Not Meant to Stand* would forever be the play not meant to be. The audience was restive in its discontent. At intermission it was clear that the play was not only not hitting home, but that the audience had taken an active dislike to it. It was an ugly play filled with mostly ugly people. But that was Tennessee's life at the time and this was his statement of account.

As Aaron Gold had predicted, the NBC taping was clothed in impenetrable security. Catching sight of me, Tennessee beckoned me in. As I stood talking to him, a producer for the show came up and asked if I was a close member of the family. Thinking to make a joke, Tennessee said, "Anything but that!" The crew person then informed me that I had to leave the set. As I turned to go, Tennessee grabbed my hand. "I'll be there, baby. Write down the name of that restaurant and the address for me. I've got so much on my mind right now. These people are angling for a premature burial in more ways than one."

I paced the Goodman lobby for an hour and then took a cab to Biggs, the restaurant whose owner, Peter Salchow, had graciously agreed to keep open to any hour in order to accommodate the meeting. Falls was already there, a great bear of a man, kind of hunkered down over our table at the window. I wondered how long he would be forced to wait.

After perhaps an hour and a half I was paged to the phone. The other dining rooms of the Victorian mansion in which the restaurant was housed were all darkened and still. Service lights alone illuminated some of the gilt about the ornate mirrors above the shadowed fireplaces.

It was Tennessee, in his way the ever-faithful Tennessee, on the line. "Baby, I'm at the restaurant with the big blue hat! They deny that you're within! Are you within walking distance?"

Tennessee had found himself at the restaurant next door, whose only distinguishing characteristic was the Magritte-like blue homberg it used for a logo. "The big house on the corner, Tennessee. Falls, the chef, two waiters, we're all still here waiting for you."

Soon there was the resounding rap of the heavy bronze knocker on the door. The boom echoed through the empty house. Falls looked up, startled from his one drink of the evening.

"Believe it or not, it's Tennessee, Robert."

And so it was. And in a most obliging and affable mood. He had wanted this meeting with Falls.

"Your pals in the media think they've got me hood-winked, baby. You should have stayed for the action. They couldn't have been more heavy-handed as they angled for the kind of personal detail which is only of interest to those reading of the newly dead. I know an obituary when I see one. At the end of the taping, three of your friends formed a gang which insisted I go right back to the hotel. Although we all acknowledged the hour rather late for a dinner, I assured them I was coming here to meet with you. I had to fight to get into a cab by myself."

It was well past midnight when the dinner service began. Tennessee's conversation with Robert Falls seemed an earnest one. It concluded with agreement for more communication.

"Let's have dinner alone tomorrow night, baby. I've had enough of these bullying social occasions."

CHAPTER XXVII

—⟨◦⟩—

Stage Direction: Rain

IT WAS THE NEXT night. In the dark restaurant, Tennessee held out his hand across the table and gently held mine. He continued to hold it as we talked.

"Baby, you must wonder why I keep coming back. I know it's over. Everything I do now is a kind of rehearsal for the end. I don't know when it will be. I could say that I come back because I like looking into your eyes, which I have always wanted to paint, as I said to you the first evening of our acquaintance. It was not the flesh, but the eyes I met when I met you. You know that the eyes are allegedly the window to . . ."

After the morning critics' notices, I had expected Tennessee to be sad, angry, somber, but not particularly elegiac. But such seemed his mood. It was especially surprising because he had left me an amusing note at his hotel that morning. "We shall have to call them 'mourning' critics now, baby. See you at dinner."

257

Seeking to cheer the mood, I asked, "How did you like Robert Falls? Do you see any potential there?"

"For a man of the theatre, he's unusually taciturn, you know. I had to do most of the talking. But I liked what I saw. I plan to invite him down to Key West for further talks."

"Tennessee, why don't we make some tapes of you reading some of your most famous roles? They'd be a great gift to the theatre. A kind of definitive reading for posterity."

"You've caught the obit bug, baby? It's really in the wind, isn't it?"

"It's just that there's such a paucity of recordings from you. Your readings are extraordinary. Why not do readings from *Streetcar; Cat; Suddenly Last Summer?*"

"You see yourself as Dr. Cukrowicz and me as Mrs. Venable? I'll do it if you'll do it."

"No, Tennessee, seriously, all roles as read by you."

"The female roles as well? Me as Blanche?"

"You were virtually doing her at *Streetcar* the other day. Why not?"

"Because I'm a man, baby. The male gender. I don't read female roles." He was curiously upset at the suggestion, although it had almost certainly been proposed before.

This was to prove another project not destined for fulfillment. He seemed not to want to discuss it further.

"I've invited the great black mystic to join us for dinner, baby. I'm afraid he's just about worn out his magic as far as I'm concerned, but don't tell him that. Don't ever let anyone make fun of him. He's sincere."

"I thought we could just be alone to talk tonight, Tennessee. Who else did you invite?"

"Just a gay boy I met in Key West. I slipped on the steps of the Monster and he kept me from falling."

"And now he's being rewarded in the manner of the gods?"

"I know you don't like these people, but I thought some kind of recognition was appropriate for the service he rendered me."

The black minister arrived. And shortly thereafter the young man who had entered Tennessee's private mythology as a savior.

We arranged ourselves about the table. The black minister attempted to speak in seer-like ways, but his attempts fell on deaf ears. The young man tried to get his oar in, but was patted on the arm by Tennessee and became silent. Tennessee was truly awkward. He seemed embarrassed.

And I came to feel that I had nothing more I wished to say to anyone at the table.

Dinner was perfunctory. Everyone was impatient to go.

And then we stood together on the parking lot pavement wet from the Chicago rain.

"I love you, Tennessee," I said.

"I don't know why, baby. I don't know why," he replied.

Our relationship had taken so many body blows that I could no longer answer him. But it was true.

I bowed my head to his brow and kissed his temple. And that was goodbye. Once again, fellow St. Louis poet/playwright T.S. Eliot had called it. April was the cruelest month.

EPILOG

―――――――――― ❧ ――――――――――

TENNESSEE WILLIAMS DIED NINE months after our last
meeting. After the unsuccessful production of *A House Not
Meant to Stand,* he returned to Key West. His life in the
professional theatre was over.

I heard occasional reports of him. He was in Sicily, where
he astounded a casual journalist who asked what he was
writing about by saying, "Exploding volcanoes!" I'm sure
the journalist didn't get it. And then he was in New York
where, stopped on the street by a mutual friend, he asked
about Elia Kazan. "Tell him to keep writing," he said.

It was not astonishing that Marlon Brando, whom Tennessee always regarded as America's greatest actor, had the
last best things to say about Tennessee on the occasion of
his death:

"By the time death came he had been so close to it so
many times psychologically, emotionally, and physically
that it was probably just a shave and a haircut to him.

261

"We are all diminished by his death. Lessened by his passing. If we had a culture that gave support and assistance to a man of his delicacy, perhaps he could have survived. There is no real solace or cultural support for artists who find it difficult to find root in this culture, which is so hard and fast and commercial."

Brando concluded: "His was a wounded life."

As at first a stranger and then as a friend, I and a few others tried to provide the solace and understanding the culture could not provide.

"Make voyages, attempt things," Tennessee had written in *Camino Real,* a play written when Methedrine could still merge successfully with the dream. And so we who had come to know him came to see, the chaos of his private world became as ungovernable as the public world of his ironic tragedies. No longer able to achieve or even bear the intensity of his creation, he had let his life at the end play out inseparable from his drama.

With the creativity, that is to say the life that was left to him, he burnt his stages with the seeming contempt of an about-to-be-exiled king.

In this dramatic mode, he wanted to tell the world one last time what he had to say and to do so he had to avoid the lingering death he so feared. He must die quickly.

He could still summon the muse of ironic tragedy one last time and certainly did so when he checked into the Sunset Suite at the Elysee Hotel in Manhattan. His dark euphemism for death through his last years had been "checking out." In summoning the stage directions for his last work, of which he had already provided the words, he would need a hotel with a resonant name. Elysee, how like Elysian.

It was the quiet streetcar of his own desire that moved inexorably to these fields, its destination tracked long since, with this last stop the starting point for all the other plays that had gone before.